A Survivor's Guide To Successful Aging

With recipes for 1 week
provided by Christina Schilling

Dr. Ray M. Schilling, MD

ISBN: 1494765330
ISBN 13: 9781494765330
Library of Congress Control Number: 2013923502
CreateSpace Independent Publishing Platform
North Charleston, South Carolina

Dedication:

I dedicate this book to those who are willing to work on prevention in order to achieve a longer life without disabilities.

Acknowledgement:

I like to thank the staff from CreateSpace for their valuable input in helping with editing and publishing this book. My granddaughter, Taylor, put a lot of thought and technical help into the design of the book cover; thank you, Taylor! I like to thank my wife for supporting me throughout this project and for contributing to the book by writing the recipe section. She also helped with proofreading when my language turned too medical.

Contents

Contents

Introduction

My background

Medicine is a fascinating topic. Health and wellness are buzzwords, and magazines and Internet publications have disseminated vast amounts of information that are readily available. So it should be easy for anybody to get the important facts that tell us how our bodies work, how we take care of our day to day health and how to stay well. It does sound uncomplicated, but even though our bodies are the same model that existed thousands of years ago, we are now inundated with new data: genetics are starting to get demystified, our immune system has become almost like a new universe of medicine, nerve pathways are being decoded, and research has taken giant steps forward in the last 50 years.

I had completed my medical training and my internship in a traditional medical school in Germany. After studying medicine I relocated to Canada and spent a few years doing cancer research at the Ontario Cancer Institute in Toronto, Ontario.

There was a brief detour at McMaster University in Hamilton, Ontario where I got introduced to the problem-oriented approach to medicine and passed the Canadian State examination.

I started to practice medicine in my family practice in a small town of Southern British Columbia. My senior associate had a wealth of practical knowledge that he was happy to share with me. He could uncannily diagnose a patient who presented with acute appendicitis by close observation before the laboratory tests confirmed his suspicion. I understood more and more that medicine was not strictly a science, but also an art. As I looked after patients over the years I noticed that very often the problems of the aging population was a study of human suffering. One patient stated: "The golden years, doc? I tell you, the golden years are for the birds!" Prevention had not become the word that was in everybody's mouth. I knew about vitamin supplements, and recommended vitamin E for heart health, which resulted in snarky remarks from some of my more conservative older colleagues.

I came to the conclusion that any disease would be better prevented before it could wreak havoc with the health of a patient. Over the sixteen years of my family practice in Langley, B.C. I believed in prevention. I encouraged my patients to do everything that was known at the time to prevent obesity, high blood pressure and manage stress through relaxation techniques. It was gratifying to see success! In many instances patients were able to get back to normal blood pressure readings or managed to successfully combat diabetes with dietary and other lifestyle changes. In the second phase of my career I dealt with occupational medicine. It was often obvious how problematic lifestyles paved the way to arthritic changes and back problems. In these cases prevention was too late, and the only choice was conventional curative medicine. I was still involved in treating patients in a walk- in clinic setting. However, there was a time constraint in examining and talking to patients. Yet it was very clear that patients had questions that could not be dealt with in a 5 to 10 minute visit. My next project became a medical website that would be accessible to everybody and give medical information in everyday language. This is how www.nethealthbook.com and also a medical blog, www.askdrray.com were started. During all the years of practicing medicine I found out more about medical research at conferences for continuing medical education, but there were also new pathways in medicine. A small group of physicians had founded the A4M, the American Academy of Anti Aging Medicine. The number of the A4M members increased dramatically over the years to 26,000 physicians in 2013. I joined them as a member in 2008. I became curious about the conferences that were organized by A4M and have since attended A4M conference in Las Vegas every year.

My own experience with anti-aging medicine:

In February of 2001, my wife and I attended an antiaging conference in San Diego. The keynote speaker was Dr. Barry Sears, the inventor of the Zone diet. Having read a book by him before the conference, we were excited to hear him speak in person. We liked the book; we liked the talk. So we cut out sugar and starchy foods and stuck to a diet with the calories deriving 50 percent from low-glycemic complex carbohydrates and 25 to 30 percent from lean meat, poultry, and fish. We reduced our calories derived from fat to about 15 to 20 percent (there is hidden fat even in lean meat). In place of butter, we began to eat low-fat cheeses and use olive oil for cooking and in salad dressings. We both shed fifty pounds within three months without any hunger pangs. Our energy increased and has stayed elevated ever since. We had no problem getting our body mass index (BMI) down to 23.5 or 24.0, which is usually viewed as normal by the medical profession. We noticed, however, that when we did not exercise, we had a problem maintaining our normal weight. So we took up ballroom dancing, having been inspired by *Dancing with the Stars*. That was six years ago.

Four years ago our energy levels were slowly going down, particularly after a long night of dancing. Hormone tests revealed the initial stages of age-related hormone deficiencies, which did not come as a surprise. Decreasing hormone levels had been discussed in detail at the conference in San Diego in 2001, and we had heard the same at the other antiaging conferences we'd attended each year from 2009 onward. Thanks to bioidentical hormone replacements, these levels normalized within one year. Our energy was back, and our weight stayed normal.

As I became curious, whether the steps to wellness I had taken where really all that was necessary, I read more. And there was lots of more information! In 2008 I read Suzanne Somers's book *Breakthrough*. It contained a chapter about detoxification that explained that tuna and other big game fish contained mercury. We decided that we wanted to know whether we might have some mercury on board. We had urine tests for toxic metals and were shocked to learn that we had noticeable levels of mercury and lead. We cut our fish consumption from three to four times per week down to once or twice per week. In order to remove the accumulated mercury and other heavy metals, we started intravenous chelation treatments with vitamin C (10 g) and glutathione (1,250 mg) every two weeks, which is a more gentle method of chelation therapy that is used with autistic children. In July 2012 the Canadian media reported findings of radioactive salmon from Japan's nuclear disaster earlier that year. After hearing this news, we stopped eating all fish and other seafood, not only because of radioactivity, but also because of other toxins like mercury, cadmium, and PCBs. Instead we take high doses of molecularly distilled omega-3 fatty acids along with our other supplements. In addition, we also started eating mostly organic foods, as we do not want to ingest insecticides, herbicides, and other toxins.

We acquired body composition scales, which give information about visceral fat percentage, muscle mass percentage, BMI, weight, and the basic metabolic rate. When we noticed that our dance program was not good enough to lower our BMI below about 23.5, we introduced a one-hour gym program consisting of thirty minutes on the treadmill, fifteen minutes of upper-body circuits, and fifteen minutes of lower-body circuits every day. Any dance activity would be just an additional exercise on top of this base exercise from the gym. It took only about two months before our fat composition decreased, our muscle mass increased, our visceral fat went to normal (at 5 percent), and our BMI stabilized in the 21.5 to 22.0 range. We feel a lot more confident about staying healthy without really thinking much about the weight. It is now a routine we follow, the way an athlete would to stay in shape. While nobody has a permanent guarantee of everlasting health, we made these lifestyle changes in the hope of preventing diseases and conditions we do not need in our retirement, like diabetes, arthritis, heart attacks, strokes, cancer, and Alzheimer's.

What we did not know until after the 20th A4M Anti-Aging Conference in Las Vegas (mid-December 2012) was that inadvertently we had been protected from exposure to chemically modified wheat from 2001 onward, as we had cut out wheat from our diet and avoided starchy foods. Unfortunately many Americans still expose themselves unknowingly to unknown quantities of this modified wheat and, as a result, suffer from leaky gut syndrome with the associated changes in the immune system and the development of autoimmune diseases. Sugar and starch overconsumption add to weight-management problems as the liver simply changes the calories into fat, which is stored as belly fat and fat under the skin.

About this book:

In this book I have compiled what I believe you should know about managing your weight, negotiating the cholesterol and fat question, and staying active and healthy into a ripe old age without disabilities or Alzheimer's disease. It can be done.

In chapter 1 I describe the metabolic changes that are associated with obesity, called the metabolic syndrome.

In chapter 2 I am discussing the risk factors associated with the metabolic syndrome. The Framingham Heart Study is cited as it has analyzed mortality data in relation to the number of risk factors we are exposed to.

Chapter 3 reviews the health consequences of the metabolic syndrome and lays the foundation to prevention.

The next 5 chapters deal with risk factors in more detail and tell you how to use them in your favor.

Chapter 4 deals with food as an important factor of prevention. You will learn that sugar and starch are high risk factors undermining your health and that the high carb/low fat diet recommendation is outdated. Instead I recommend a low carb/medium healthy fat diet in its place.

Engaging in a regular exercise program can prevent half of the major diseases and I discuss this in chapter 5.

We all know that stress can be a killer; chapter 6 deals with this and with what you can do to avoid it.

In chapter 7 I explain the effects of hormones and what the lack of them can do. This is a topic that is often ignored by mainstream medicine except for thyroid problems and diabetes. But we have many more hormones and they too need to be balanced. Hormone deficiencies have to be determined by blood and/or saliva hormone tests and corrected with bioidentical hormones. Many people have reservations about hormone treatments as large trials showed detrimental effects with synthetic hormones. I explain in detail the difference between synthetic hormones and bioidentical hormones. The former make you sick, the latter extend your life.

Chapter 8 explains why we need certain vitamins and supplements. Harvard University researchers were the first team to study the effects of vitamins on disease prevention. Antioxidants are required to stop free radicals from attacking your DNA. Anti-inflammatory supplements like CoQ-10, omega-3 and vitamin D3 are keeping LDL cholesterol from getting oxidized. LDL cholesterol is the transport form of cholesterol that is produced in the liver and is meant to safely reach your vital organs, the heart and the brain to provide them with the material to replace membranes and cells.

Chapter 9 and 10 describe how to change your lifestyle habits and how to monitor them once you did.

Chapter 11 explains that with the reduction of risk factors come real benefits of preventing the major disabling diseases, entering into your golden age without pains, walkers, wheelchairs or being admitted to a nursing home.

Finally in an appendix you can find 7 days of recipes for breakfasts, lunches, dinners, desserts and snacks, compiled by my wife, Christina Schilling, who is an exceptional cook. Christina operated a bed and breakfast for 15 years and beside the breakfasts also offered dinners to guests who were interested in it. German type cooking has been replaced by an international variety of organic foods with emphasis on freshness and easy preparation.

Enjoy your health. Enjoy a longer, active life!

Chapter 1:
The Metabolic Syndrome

In 1969 the executive board of the World Health Organization made the following statement: "Coronary Heart Disease has reached enormous proportions, striking more and more at younger subjects. It will result in coming years in the greatest epidemic mankind has faced unless we are able to reverse the trend by concentrated research into its cause and prevention."

These prophetic words unfortunately have come true. The Framingham Heart Study and many other studies have been able to pinpoint the causes of the increase in heart disease, but people have not reversed the trend (The Framingham Heart Study). It is one thing to know the causes, and it is another to convince the public about the importance of prevention. Soon the baby boomers and the public at large will have no choice but to embrace the concept of prevention, as curative medicine will not be able to deliver the goods when it comes to replacing damaged arteries.

Since 1969 extensive research has been done. And in the midnineties, physicians became aware that what the World Health Organization had feared had become a full-blown reality. People in the Western world were in a health crisis, suffering from increasing obesity and dying by the millions from heart attacks and strokes. Conventional medicine often just treats symptoms without addressing the underlying lifestyle problems aggressively. Conventional practitioners also are under the influence of Big Pharma who support treating symptoms only with expensive prescription drugs. This leads to ever-increasing health care budgets without changing the underlying causes of the patients afflicted by the metabolic syndrome.

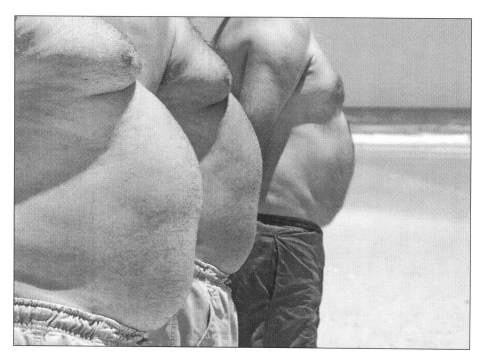

Profound changes occur in the metabolism when a person is gaining weight and becoming obese. These changes lead to health consequences such as premature heart attacks, strokes, type 2 diabetes, arthritis, osteoporosis, hip fractures, infertility, high blood pressure, cancer, autoimmune diseases, neurological illnesses, and others. The good news is that it is relatively simple to turn this trend around by watching what you eat, getting into a regular physical fitness routine, and changing your attitude about life in general. Later in this book, I will explain in detail how this can be done.

In the last few decades, doctors and researchers have concentrated on investigating the syndrome of insulin resistance—originally dubbed *syndrome X*, but renamed *metabolic syndrome*—in more detail. You will still hear all of these names, which are simply synonyms; we will use the newer term, metabolic syndrome. One common condition where the metabolism is changed is diabetes and it is not surprising that there is an overlap between patients who are just obese and have the metabolic syndrome only and others who in addition develop diabetes. Diabetes often develops in a person whose food intake reflects poor choices, including overconsumption of calories. Many such people take in large amounts of refined carbohydrates, such as foods high in starch and sugar, as well as excessive amounts of fat. In addition, these higher-weight people tend to not exercise enough and therefore do not burn enough calories. The excess calories are stored as glycogen, the storage form of sugar, in the liver and the muscles. When the glycogen storage space of the liver and the muscles is full, the liver metabolizes any excess sugar into triglycerides and cholesterol for storage as fat in the abdomen, under the skin, and in the organs. Fat is also deposited in the arterial walls, leading to heart attacks and strokes.

Both sugar and fat require insulin to be transported through the cell membranes for storage. In the early stages of the metabolic syndrome, a condition called hyperinsulinism occurs, in which the pancreas produces more than the average amount of insulin. Eventually the individual develops the metabolic syndrome. The process behind it explains why researchers originally considered it the syndrome of insulin resistance. The word *resistance* in this context refers to insulin receptors on cell surfaces that, in view of high sugar or triglyceride levels, become less expressed, creating a slowing down, or resistance to, being absorbed by cells. This results in insulin overproduction, but there is a limit to how much insulin the body can produce. When the patient's pancreas runs out of insulin supply, blood sugars are elevated, and the doctor diagnoses the person as diabetic. It is important to recognize that at the time of a diabetes diagnosis, the blood vessels have already been damaged for several years, becoming so during the time of insulin resistance when the pancreas produced too much insulin but the blood sugars were still normal or only mildly elevated. Another condition, which affects women, is called polycystic ovary syndrome (cysts of the ovaries with missing periods). This is also the result of insulin resistance, and these women are often infertile. We know from other literature that female patients with diabetes also often develop polycystic ovary syndrome.

Here is a visual summary of the conditions common in the metabolic syndrome:

COMMON ELEMENTS OF THE METABOLIC SYNDROME

Diabetes (adult onset)	High blood pressure	Obesity
High blood fat levels	Hardening of arteries	Cysts in the ovaries

The good news is that these conditions are not here to stay. In the early stages, they can be brought back to normal. The body does best when the metabolic processes are balanced. This way the blood sugar levels are normal, the circulating fatty substances in the blood (i.e., triglycerides and cholesterol) are nondamaging to arteries, and the blood pressure is stable. When all of the body's hormones are balanced, they are able to send proper signals to the organs. As a result, the machinery of the body will function smoothly, and the individual will age at a slower rate. If we are willing to remove a few risk factors, we can make such improvements.

These facts are not new. We know that those who quit smoking or who have never smoked cigarettes in their lives will prevent lung cancer and a host of other cancers and reduce the risk of heart attacks and strokes. It is not surprising that those who do not smoke cigarettes live longer and stay healthier. What was not known until recently is that other lifestyle factors also contribute profoundly to our well-being and to the probability of a longer life. In her 1974 cookbook Dr. Ethel Nelson, a pathologist in Stoneham, Massachusetts, wrote the following:

> I have been greatly impressed with the importance of correct diet in the prevention of the degenerative diseases, which are so common in our world today. I am speaking especially of atherosclerosis, or hardening of the arteries, with its effect on, not only the aorta (the greatest artery of the body), but also the coronaries (arteries of the heart) and cerebral vessels (arteries of the brain) as well. It is well recognized now that the eating habits of the average American are contributing to many pathological states.

Dr. Nelson's remarks are as fresh and true today as they were back in 1974. I will deal with some of the research that has been collected since then. I will also deal with new insights that show that we can significantly contribute to our well-being by eating sensibly and staying physically active. Another part of changing for the better involves assessing your body chemistry, including your hormone status, on an ongoing basis to monitor your progress. You will need a health practitioner who is willing to work with you, specifically a naturopathic doctor or an anitaging physician knowledgeable in bioidentical hormone assessments. You may be surprised that you can prevent disabilities and diseases that people have traditionally associated with aging. At the core of this book is the knowledge about food, the metabolic syndrome, and the ways to normalize the metabolism and the aging hormone status that will allow you to do so.

Brief historic overview of the metabolic syndrome

In 1936 a doctor observed that adults who were obese could develop diabetes and yet have enough circulating insulin in their blood (Ng, D.S., 2003). Up to that point, physicians only knew that a lack of insulin production in the pancreas would lead to diabetes, which we now call type 1 diabetes; with this type of diabetes the pancreas no longer produces insulin. From then on it was noted that the pancreas could still produce insulin despite diabetes, particularly when patients were obese, and this was called type 2 diabetes. Later research coined this *insulin resistance,* which, as I explained earlier, comes from an adaptive response of the cells that are expressing fewer insulin receptors on their membrane surfaces, meaning that more insulin is necessary to transport glucose across the cell membranes. This results in a relative loss of power of the insulin (insulin sensitivity), and the patient becomes diabetic. In 1988 further observations about insulin resistance were made when a clustering of a variety of risk factors were noted in patients with insulin resistance. Instead of continuing to diagnose patients with "syndrome X," as physicians had originally coined it, they decided to diagnose them with "syndrome of insulin resistance"(Reaven, G., 1988). The following risk factors were known at that time to be associated with this syndrome: high blood pressure or diabetes, a low level of the high-density lipoprotein of cholesterol (HDL), and a high triglyceride blood level. The presence of any of these factors that were part of the full syndrome of insulin resistance were known to be associated with a higher risk for heart attacks.

Research done in the nineties showed profound metabolic changes in the bodies of people who had the syndrome of insulin resistance. Other diseases were also linked with the condition. Two thorough reviews were published—the first by the World Health Organization in 1999 and the second published by an Expert Panel in JAMA 2001—that suggested that a better name for this metabolic state in which major diseases were being incubated would be "metabolic syndrome." As I summarized in a blog in July 2003, there was a consensus among researchers that when three or more of the five risk factors were present in a given patient, the metabolic syndrome was present. Below I am listing the five risk factors in tabular form. It is based on the *Third Report of the National Cholesterol Education Program Expert Panel*, which was revised in November of 2002.

ELEMENTS LEADING TO DIAGNOSIS OF "METABOLIC SYNDROME"

FINDING	COMMENTS
Abdominal obesity (waist circumference)	> 102 cm (40") in men > 88 cm (34.5") in women
Elevated triglyceride level	150 mg/dl (1.70 mmol/L) or higher
Low HDL cholesterol level	< 40 mg/dl (1.04 mmol/L) in men < 50 mg/dl (1.29 mmol/L) in women
Elevated blood pressure	Systolic or diastolic pressure > 130/85 mm Hg
High fasting blood glucose level	Fasting glucose > 110 mg/dl (6.1 mmol/L)

So why is metabolic syndrome considered present when three or more findings of this table are present? Perhaps I can compare this best with a power failure in your kitchen: one of the electrical circuits must be responsible when you notice that a light, the fridge, and the microwave are not working. In other words, we can correctly conclude that if a certain constellation of observations occurs, there likely is a reason behind it. I am attempting in this book to explain the reasons for good health and the reasons for poor health. Fortunately, you do not need to be an electrician or sort out any circuits. You also do not need to be a physician to take care of your health, though using a family doctor to identify your particular risk factors can be helpful. With the help of the advice later in the book, you will be able to take charge of the lifestyle factors that you need to change.

Chapter 2:
The Risk Factors Associated with the Metabolic Syndrome

The metabolic syndrome seems to be more frequent in the older population. One study reported that only 7 percent of participants aged twenty to twenty-nine had the metabolic syndrome while 40 percent of participants aged seventy or older were affected. In addition to age, other factors play a role. It is thought that too many calories coupled with too little activity over a long period of time, perhaps coupled in some people with a genetic tendency to develop the metabolic syndrome, leads to an accumulation of fat around and inside of the abdomen, or visceral fat. Because fat cells have their own hormone systems, this accumulation causes a change in an individual's metabolism, including elevation of the insulin level with associated loss of insulin sensitivity. The more obese a person becomes, the less effective insulin becomes in transporting blood sugar through cell walls. At the same time, the liver metabolism is changing, producing less of the good cholesterol (HDL) and overproducing LDL cholesterol; LDL is oxidized when the blood sugar level is too high, which is the case in prediabetic and diabetic patients. Oxidized LDL is highly unstable and functions as a free radical, which is taken up by macrophages from the blood. Once the macrophages engulf the oxidized LDL, they puff up and are now called foam cells; they are deposited into the lining of the arteries. From there the entrapped foam cells send cytokines into the bloodstream. This attracts more oxidized LDL and leads to more inflammation of the lining of the arteries.

These fat deposits in the arteries—particularly in the coronary arteries—shorten life by leading to heart attacks and strokes (see "The New York Times Hardening of the Arteries In-Depth Report"). The metabolic changes associated with the metabolic syndrome stimulate the liver to produce a different mix of coagulation factors, and this leads to a tendency to form clots in arteries, the veins of the legs, and the lungs. After a number of years, the pancreas gets exhausted from producing extra insulin. The patient eventually develops diabetes, which means there is a relative lack of insulin. In a person with diabetes, the metabolic changes lead to elevated cholesterol, elevated triglycerides, accelerated hardening of the arteries, and a higher risk that the coronary arteries will clog up. Whoever is overweight or obese and has the metabolic syndrome has a higher risk of dying from a severe heart attack at any time. A normal weight population (body mass index below 25.0) does not have this risk.

The Framingham Heart Study has been tracking these health issues for decades. Researchers followed a large number of obese and men and women and a control group with normal body weight for sixteen years who were part of the Framingham study. They kept track of the death rates from heart attacks and found that the risk of dying from a heart attack was higher among those who had more than three risk factors and highest when more than five risk factors were present. Before I list these, I like to explain that physicians have established that you can use an electrocardiogram tracing (ECG), which measures ECG strain as a reliable predictor for the negative effect from an increase of blood pressure on the heart muscle.

The five risk factors for developing heart attacks evaluated were height and weight (BMI), smoking habits, electrocardiogram tracing (ECG), blood cholesterol subfractions (the "good" HDL cholesterol and the "bad" LDL cholesterol), and blood sugar levels (more recently also the hemoglobin A1C level) to check for diabetes. The following table is a summary of the relative risk ratios for each of these five risk factors.

TABLE 1 RELATIVE RISK FOR DYING FROM A HEART ATTACK OVER A PERIOD OF SIXTEEN YEARS (ONE RISK FACTOR)

RISK FACTOR	MALE	FEMALE
None	1.0	1.0
HDL < 35 mg/dL	1.49	1.67
Diabetes	1.94	1.85
Smoker	1.93	2.78
ECG strain (blood pressure high)	2.58	1.66
Obesity (BMI > 30.0)	1.66	1.64

Essentially this table shows that each of these independent risk factors can be measured. The lowest risk is assigned a scale of 1-fold, meaning there is no increased risk, as mathematically a number multiplied by one is the same value as the number. Researchers observed two oddities. First, smoking led to a higher death rate in women (2.78-fold when compared to women who did not smoke) than in men (1.93-fold when compared to nonsmoking men). Also, high blood pressure led to a higher death rate in men than in women, as men with ECG strain due to high blood pressure had a death rate that was 2.58-fold higher than men with normal blood pressure. Women with the same signs of ECG strain from high blood pressure had only a 1.66-fold higher death rate than women with normal blood pressure.

At this point we need you to remember that risks for development of heart attacks can be measured only by observing large populations like that of the ongoing Framingham Heart Study.

When this method of risk calculation is done with groups of people who were exposed to three or more risk factors, differences compared to those without risk factors really show. The authors of the above-mentioned study made the observation that particularly when three or more risk factors were combined in the same patient, there were significant risks to such patients of dying from a heart attack. This is shown in the next table.

TABLE 2 RELATIVE RISK OF DYING FROM HEART ATTACK OVER A PERIOD OF SIXTEEN YEARS (MORE THAN ONE RISK FACTOR)

RISK FACTORS	MALE	FEMALE
None	1.0	1.0
Obesity + smoking	3.2	4.56
Obesity + smoking + diabetes	6.2	8.43
Obesity + smoking + diabetes + ECG strain	16.0	14.0
Obesity + smoking + diabetes + ECG strain + HDL<35 mg/dL	23.8	23.4

Regarding this table it is important to note that risk factors that are present in the same patient are multiplied, not added, to determine the overall risk for dying from a heart attack. The values in table 2 show the individual's overall risk for dying of a heart attack by multiplying the appropriate risk factors from table 1. As can be seen from groups 2, 3, and 4, where three to five risks are present, any person in one of these groups has a very significant overall risk to die from a heart attack.

When all five risk factors are present (i.e., an obese person with diabetes and uncontrolled high blood pressure who smokes and has a low HDL cholesterol), the risk for death from a heart attack within sixteen years would be more than 23-fold higher than that of a normal-weight person who does not smoke and is otherwise healthy. For clarity I have depicted the four risk groups from table 2 as a bar graph below (figure1). The numbers of the risk groups correspond with the numbers of table 2. You can clearly see that adding another risk factor significantly increases the risk of dying from a heart attack. Group 4 (which has five risk factors) is significantly different from group 3. However, if a person from group 4 decides to go for regular walks, which can actually increase the HDL cholesterol above 35 mg/dL, the risk over the next sixteen years will be reduced to that of group 3. This is the basis of risk intervention, which will be discussed later in chapter 11.

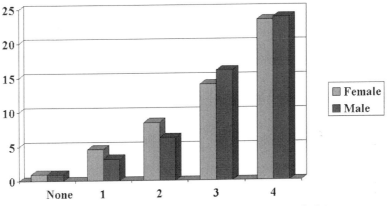

Figure 1 Relative risk of dying from heart attack over a period of sixteen years (more than one risk)

A research group from the Netherlands compiled data from the Framingham Heart Study at the forty-year follow-up point, which I cited in my January 2003 blog. The sample discussed was a group of obese smokers. They lost on average more than thirteen years of life (regardless of sex) compared to the nonsmokers with a normal body weight. Fig. 2 shows the results of that study as a bar graph.

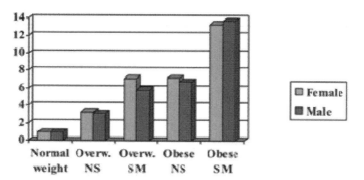

Figure 2 Years of life lost forty years after the Framingham Heart Study was started (Overw.=overweight, NS=nonsmoker, SM=smoker)

In other words, forty years ago a nonsmoker with a normal body weight had a general life expectancy of eighty-five, but in the case of an obese smoker, the average age of death was seventy-two. This translates the somewhat abstract figures in table 2 into the harsh reality that is associated with a certain lifestyle. This combination of only two risk factors, which is associated with a 3- to 4-fold risk over sixteen years of dying from a heart attack (group1 in figure1), actually led to thirteen years of loss of life when averaged over forty years (obese SM group in figure 2). This means that many more people with multiple risk factors will die from heart attacks—perhaps twenty or thirty years earlier—if this is ignored. Although heart attacks are one of the major causes of death in obese people, this is by no means the only health risk. A medical review article has listed all of the major medical complications of obesity (Margellos-Anast, 2008). Apart from diabetes and heart attacks, there is a significant risk for other vascular diseases, such as strokes, high blood pressure, kidney disease, and loss of eyesight. Several cancers, such as colon cancer, breast cancer in women, and prostate cancer in men, also appear to be more common in obese people. In addition health conditions such as reflux esophagitis (GERD), gallstone disease, and liver disease are more common. Lung problems, too, are more common in the obese; these include sleep apnea, breathing problems, and susceptibility to flus and lung infections. Knee osteoarthritis, hip fractures, carpal tunnel syndrome, and disc herniations in the spine are just a few of the complications of obesity regarding the muscles and bones. As indicated above, obese women also experience fertility problems due to polycystic ovary syndrome. There are also risks during pregnancy to both the fetus and the pregnant obese woman due to gestational diabetes, gestational hypertension, preeclampsia, and complicated deliveries with an increased C-section rate. Close supervision by the treating physician and obstetrician is necessary in these cases.

Due to these additional risks, the actual death rate from all causes due to obesity is higher than the values given above, which account for deaths from heart attacks only.

Heart attacks are only one manifestation in patients with severe hardening of the arteries. Strokes are another manifestation of this and occur also frequently in obese patients. In an article that I reviewed in my December 2002 blog, the authors noticed a risk factor of 1.9-fold for strokes in obese male physicians in the United States who were followed for twelve and a half years (see short summary below).

Obesity (excessive weight) a predictor of high risk for stroke:

After all this gloomy news, what is the good news? The Third Report of the National Cholesterol Education Program Expert Panel in 2002 states that for every 2 percent weight reduction in obese women, there is a 4 percent reduction in the risk for heart attacks. Again, this study went on for sixteen years. Over forty years or longer, the effect would be even greater. You may ask what about the risk reduction for men? The answer is that in this particular study the report was based on clinical trials that were done only with women, but common sense tells you that for men the reduction is likely very similar as in table 1 above the risks for heart attacks from obesity for both sexes was also very similar.

What can we learn from this? The earlier we intervene with any of the risk factors mentioned above and the more successful we are in conquering as many of these as possible, the healthier we will be and the longer we will live. Not only will we live longer, but we will enjoy life more fully. The odds are in our favor that we will be out on the dance floor at the age of seventy and eighty rather than disabled in a nursing home.

The effect of obesity on the development of stroke later in life was the subject of a study in which 21,414 male physicians from the United States were followed for 12.5 years. At that point there were 747 strokes. The authors found that the rates of strokes were in direct relation to the amount of excessive weight. In other words, the higher the weight, the higher the risk to develop a stroke. A BMI above 30 was always associated with a 1.9-fold risk to develop a stroke, compared to normal weight controls (BMI less than 25). The obesity-dependent risk to develop a stroke was independent from other risk factors such as diabetes, high cholesterol, or high blood pressure. Dr. Kurth from the Brigham and Women's Hospital, Boston, said that this finding is very significant in view of the fact that many young adults in the United States are either overweight or obese, which means they will be exposed to this risk for a longer period of time than adults. This would increase the risk to develop strokes even further, particularly later in life. He hopes that physicians will concentrate on treating obesity more aggressively in order to prevent strokes. In industrial countries, strokes are the main cause of disability and are ranked third on the list of causes of death in general.

Source: Arch Intern Med 2002; 162:2557-2562.

Chapter 3:
Health Consequences of the Metabolic Syndrome

1. *Why do so many people get the metabolic syndrome?*

Why is the metabolic syndrome so prevalent? As mentioned in the beginning of chapter 2, in one study only 7 percent of individuals in their twenties had the metabolic syndrome, but 40 percent of study participants aged seventy or older had it. Why? The difference was that a significant proportion of the older population had accumulated large amounts of fat, many having increased their BMI to above 25.0 (overweight) and a fair number even above 30.0 (obese).

The first reason for this is that we like to use the car or, due to distances, are forced to use it instead of walking. Our remote ancestors who were hunters and gatherers were frequently walking and running, so they burned far more calories. In the last few decades, television has made us even more sedentary, and computers have only added to this problem. We may not realize it, but we have inadvertently taken much of our previous physical activity out of our lifestyles by watching movies and television, researching problems using the computer, or playing computer games. The simple answer to this is to consciously make enough time during the day to exercise for at least thirty minutes. This could mean walking, swimming, or running or, better still, going to the gym.

The second reason for the accumulation of fat when we get older comes from the food that we eat in a twenty-four-hour period, but also from hormonal changes (low thyroid, low progesterone in women, low testosterone in men as we age). A lack of these anabolic hormones leads to accumulation of extra weight. Also, with age come certain food habits that are more entrenched than in younger people. This includes the calories in drinks as well, both soft drinks and alcoholic drinks. As we will learn later in this book, calorie restriction without hunger is the magic way to get your weight down to a comfortable BMI in the 22.0 to 23.0 range.

Closely linked with food intake is how we handle stress in our lives. Chronic stress leads to overproduction of ACTH and cortisol, hormones that lead to fluid accumulation, stomach burning, and insulin overproduction. These metabolic changes lead to hardening of the arteries and weakening of the immune system. The stomach burning leads to a feeling of hunger and a desire to eat in order to soothe the stomachache. In addition, the increase of the insulin level that occurs in response to ingested sugars and starches is followed by a dip in blood sugar one and a half to two hours later. This condition, called reactive hypoglycemia, is associated with a powerful feeling of hunger that makes the individual want to eat anything in sight.

I have given patients the task of writing down everything they put into their mouths for two weeks. When we analyzed the list, based on the composition of the eating binges, I could almost sense how low the patient's blood sugar level was at the start of such a binge. The snacks had high sugar content (candy bars, ice cream, and the like) or consisted of bread, starch, or cookies. I explained to my patients that refined carbohydrates (pasta, white bread, and so on) are broken down into sugar in the stomach, they cause a raised blood sugar level within twenty to thirty minutes. Because of the action of insulin supplied by the pancreas low blood sugar develops that stimulates the appetite for more food. I sent some of my obese patients for hypoglycemia tests using a five-hour glucose tolerance test in the lab. It confirmed that they had developed hypoglycemia with blood sugar dips at 2 to 3 hours after the initial sugar load for the test, which mimics what is also happening with high carb food intake. It is not surprising that with these food choices, the lack of physical activity, and the overindulgence in calories, many people develop a BMI well above 25 or even 30.

The third reason for the development of the obesity in young and old is the exposure to new varieties of wheat. Dr. William Davis explains how a major chemical company from Germany (the BASF) was able to chemically modify the genes of wheat in the 1960s. (Davis, 2011). The farmers liked that the modified wheat grew with stronger roots, shorter stems, and much larger grains, as this increased the yield per acre. This wheat was patented under the name of Clearfield wheat and sold around the world. Today it accounts for almost 100 percent of all commercially grown wheat. What was not publicized at the time was that the wheat's gliadin (gluten) content increased manifold from the composition of wheat strains used for thousands of years before. Higher gliadin content means more gliadin enters the body, binds to the opiate receptors of the appetite center (although it is structurally different from opium), and causes hunger for more of the same wheat-containing products. The excess calories ingested, in this case from wheat products, are stored as fat. Fat cells, having their own hormones, produce inflammatory substances that cause diabetes, high blood pressure, heart disease, strokes, and even cancer. Further, with obesity the enzyme *aromatase* from fat cells causes elevated estrogen production. This produces estrogen dominance and results in heart disease and breast cancer in females and heart disease and prostate cancer in males.

Another component in Clearfield wheat are lectins, substances that get rid of the glue-like substance between the gut cells and can cause leaky gut syndrome. This leads to exposure of immune cells to foreign proteins from the gut, which stimulates the immune system to hyperreact with autoimmune antibodies.

The obesity wave in North America and the rest of the world started when the newly patented Clearfield wheat was introduced. Since the seventies wheat products with increased gliadin and lectin content have increased incidence of leaky gut syndrome and increased people's appetites for refined carbs and wheat products, ultimately leading to wheat addiction. Government regulations aggravated the addiction even further by strongly recommending the food pyramid (a splendid marketing pyramid for wheat consumption, as one of the recommended food groups is cereals/wheat). Dr. Davis mentions that by cutting out wheat and wheat products from your diet, you can lose 400 calories per day, which can make you shed a lot of weight (Davis, 2011).

2. *How is the metabolism changed in the body? Just give me the nuts and bolts—don't bore me with details.*

When there is a surplus of calories in the body, this energy is stored as fat. This is the result of a metabolic pathway in the liver that the body learned millions of years ago, and it works well—as long as there is no oversupply of food. Years ago when a lull came and there was not as much food around, the body would use energy from the extra fat, and the body weight would even out. Since the introduction of refrigeration, deep freezing, and other food-storage technologies in the last few decades, there has been an abundance of food available to us everywhere. Also, we burn up fewer calories, as we are more sedentary. Thus if we do not in some way monitor our overall caloric intake, we will accumulate fat and become overweight or obese.

The following is a brief description of the metabolic changes that take place in our body.

a. ***Insulin abnormalities and diabetes***. It is now clear that initially when we overload our system with refined carbohydrates (i.e., sugar and starchy foods like rice, potatoes, and pasta), the pancreas produces too much insulin. After several years of dealing with the overload, the pancreas gets exhausted and falls short of the insulin demand. At that time the blood sugars are too high; your doctor diagnoses you with type 2 diabetes.

b. ***Change of the lipid metabolism, including triglycerides and cholesterol, leading to heart attacks, strokes, and circulation problems***. The liver metabolism changes profoundly in that a different mix of cholesterol is being produced that circulates in the blood. The good cholesterol (HDL) is going down and becomes an independent risk factor in the development of heart attacks (see table 1 above). The bad cholesterol (LDL) is raised considerably, and also some other very dense and unhealthy cholesterol particles clog up the arteries. Together with a change in the fatty acid metabolism of the liver, the lining of the arteries gets clogged in the whole body, particularly in the smaller arteries. Coronary arteries in the heart, the cerebral arteries in the brain and the arteries of the lower legs are particularly affected by these changes.

c. ***High blood pressure***. There is a link between obesity and high blood pressure. It appears that hormone changes, fluid retention, and the renin system in the kidney play the major role in the causation of this. The kidney is an important detoxification organ; it keeps the body fluids cleansed. As such, it has its own special hormone system that ensures it will always be well supplied with blood. When the kidney arteries do not deliver enough blood to the kidneys, special cells in the kidney produce the hormone *renin*—which is very powerful in raising blood pressure—in order to deliver a constant supply of blood to the kidneys. This mechanism also protects the kidneys when the kidney arteries get plugged from accelerated hardening due to the metabolic syndrome. The doctor will use drugs called angiotensin inhibitors and others to lower the blood pressure in these situations.

d. ***Change in the omega-3 fatty acid metabolism and the immune system and development of cancer.*** If we do not have enough omega-3 fatty acids in our food, a metabolic pathway that leads to the production of the major steroid hormones and that also builds up the strength of the immune system will fail. The end result is that cells get the wrong signals and start growing when they should stop growing. After many years of exposure to this dysfunctional metabolism, the immune system breaks down, allowing the spontaneous cancer cells that are normally removed to stay and multiply. The person with this condition is then diagnosed with a new cancer. About eleven cancers have been linked to obesity so far: cancer of the breast, prostate, colon, uterus, esophagus, liver, pancreas, gallbladder, cervix, kidney, and ovary.

e. ***Changes in the function of the gastrointestinal tract.*** When the valve between the lower esophagus and the stomach gets leaky, some acid to goes back up into the esophagus, irritating it at the lower end. After several years, this can cause esophageal cancer, and it also puts the person at a higher risk of aspiration pneumonia. When acid is brought up during sleep and ends up in the airways, the patient often ends up in the hospital. Acid is very irritating to the sensitive lining of the airways and the lung tissue, leading to aspiration pneumonia.

Gallbladder disease is common in patients with obesity, and gallstones precipitate in the gallbladder from the higher cholesterol content in the bile. This causes gallbladder colics and often leads to the need for a cholecystectomy (surgical removal of the gallbladder). Finally, liver disease is common in obese patients, with closure of small bile ducts leading to *steatosis* (a congested condition of the liver), hepatitis, and cirrhosis of the liver.

f. ***Leptin and PYY hormones***. The insert below provides a summary of an article describing the effect of a newly detected peptide hormone from the small bowel (called by scientists the *PYY hormone*). It signals to the brain when we have had enough fat to eat. This complements the effect of the leptin hormone system, which originates from fat cells and also reports to the satiety center of the brain. It appears that the PYY hormone from the bowel reports to the brain about the daily calorie intake in our food, while the leptin system tells the brain more about our total body-fat content. We do not know all of the details yet with regard to appetite control and scientists are still attempting to find out why these appetite-suppressing mechanisms seem to be disturbed in overweight and obese persons.

British researchers have shown that the peptide hormone PYY levels were much lower in patients who were significantly obese versus normal weight controls. Dr. Stephen Bloom's research group had shown earlier that with a meal rich in calories, the gut produces the PYY hormone in such a way that the higher the number of calories in food consumed, the greater the amount PYY secreted into the bloodstream. The new finding is that these hormone signals are registered in the hypothalamic tissue, a part of the brain situated just above the pituitary gland. It has been known for a long time that a satiety center in the hypothalamus regulates weight. Now it has been appreciated that there are at least two mechanisms that register weight-related hormone signals: first, the gut-related PYY hormone that tells the brain that enough food was consumed in a meal and second, leptin hormone signals. In this case leptin is secreted from the fatty tissues in the body, which tells the satiety center of the brain that not as much food needs to be consumed when our weight has reached a certain threshold.

Dr. Aylwin, one of the British researchers, measured PYY hormone levels in a number of different groups of patients, such as patients who were obese, patients who had undergone gastric bypass surgery, and a group who only had gastric banding done. Dr. Aylwin observed that the bypass surgery group had a higher than normal response of PYY hormone release as a response to a meal. This enabled them to adhere to low-calorie meals without any hunger pangs, and this group of patients did well in terms of long-term weight control. In contrast, the group with gastric banding had a flat response curve to the stimulus of a meal with respect to the PYY hormone, as did patients with obesity. The low PYY levels in response to meals likely explains why these patients continue to eat too much and why their weight-loss efforts are more difficult.

Dr. Aylwin explained that with future research new forms of medications could be developed that mimic the effects of the PYY hormone, leading to satiety and allowing patients to control their weight easier. Currently the only effective therapy for people with excessive obesity (BMI of more than 45) is the invasive gastric bypass procedure. With a new anti-obesity medication that would have the same effect as the PYY hormone, many patients might be able to have persistent weight loss without bypass surgery. However, results of this type of research likely would take about ten years, so it would be at least that long before such a new drug would be available to the public.

Source: *The Lancet Neurology* Volume 2, Number 1, January 2003.

3. *So, what does that mean in my situation?*

Each person is different. Genetic backgrounds are different. It would be best to see a family doctor and ask what risk factors are active in you. This would involve a complete physical examination, blood tests, and perhaps some other tests as required. Often diabetes is accidentally diagnosed through blood work that a doctor has ordered. This is an important finding as it is a significant risk factor for a number of associated conditions.

Diabetes. When diabetes is present, this would need to be treated by the family doctor aggressively so that eventually the blood sugar levels return to normal and the hemoglobin A1C levels do as well. The hemoglobin A1C level, which measures the sugar content of the red blood cells, gives the physician an indication as to how well the diabetes has been controlled over the past three months. If diabetes were not controlled, the risk factors in tables 1 and 2 above would apply. Diabetes leads to complications such as kidney damage, heart vessel damage, heart failure, circulation problems of the legs with the eventual need for amputation below the knee, diabetic retinopathy, and blindness. .

Blockage of arteries (arteriosclerosis) is a consequence of the changes in fatty acids and in the shift of the composition of cholesterol (less good and more bad cholesterol). It is often found in the obese patient and is accelerated by the presence of diabetes, high blood pressure, and smoking. These changes lead to premature blockage of arteries. It is important for people to know that this process occurs in every artery in the body. As the coronary arteries that supply the heart muscle with nutrients and oxygen are relatively small, the heart is one of the high-risk organs. However, the brain vessels also are affected. Quite often the middle cerebral artery gets blocked with fatty deposits, which is when the person sustains a stroke. In the kidneys, damage to the capillaries in the filtration devices (called *glomerulae*) leads to kidney damage and eventual kidney failure, which often gets complicated by diabetic and hypertensive nephropathy. This term simply means that kidney failure is more severe and occurs earlier. Eventually this can require dialysis or a kidney transplant. Other areas of concern are involvement and softening of the aorta with advancing arteriosclerotic changes, which can lead to an aortic aneurysm with a danger of sudden collapse due to a rupture of the aortic wall. In the legs, hardening of the arteries can become so severe that the patient can only walk a block, then has to stop because of severe leg cramps. Doctors have a fancy name for this: *intermittent claudication*. In this case a cardiovascular surgeon has to determine the exact location of the blockage. In some cases the surgeon may be able to do bypass surgery with an artificial Dacron artery to overbridge the blocked artery.

High blood pressure (hypertension). When the blood pressure is elevated, the heart muscle has to work overtime; this can be measured with electrocardiograms by judging the degree of ECG strain pattern. In table 1 above, we learned that the risk for death from heart attacks over sixteen years was about threefold higher in those with elevated blood pressure than in those with normal blood pressure. Patients with uncontrolled high blood pressure also are at a significantly elevated stroke risk. The mechanism of development of a stroke in these patients is a rupture of the middle cerebral artery rather than a clot. This leads to massive bleeding into the brain, often so uncontrolled that a large percentage of these patients die.

Cancer. Obesity has been linked to a variety of cancers, as already explained. However, this risk is variable for different cancers (Margellos-Anast, 2008). A large study in the European Union found that 5 percent of all cancers were due to excessive weight. Of these, 89 percent were due to uterine cancer (39 percent), kidney cancer (25 percent), and gallbladder cancer (25 percent). The remaining 11 percent came from colon cancer, postmenopausal breast cancer, and prostate cancer. There were also gender differences: men were more susceptible to colorectal and prostate cancer while women were more susceptible to cancers of the gallbladder, breast, and ovary and uterine cancer (endometrial and cervical).

Gastrointestinal problems. As explained above, people with obesity often have an acid reflux problem and may have to take antacid medication daily to prevent complications. They are more susceptible to cancer of the lower esophagus and cancer of the upper end of the stomach. Gallbladder problems are very common, and often a laparoscopic cholecystectomy (removal of gallbladder) has to be done. Occasionally this need may be missed, to the detriment of the patient, as gallstones can perforate the gallbladder and cause leakage of bile and stones into the peritoneal cavity. This causes excruciating abdominal pain in the upper midabdomen and can lead to shock and blood poisoning (bacteria in the bloodstream). This needs to be treated in the hospital, but even with the best of treatments, a certain percentage of patients will die from this serious condition.

Other problems can come from the liver when fatty infiltration of the liver tissue leads to blockage of the small bile ducts within the liver tissue, a condition called steatosis, fatty liver, or nonalcoholic chronic liver disease. The liver tissue can also get inflamed (hepatitis) and eventually turn cirrhotic (replacement of liver tissue by fibrotic tissue).

Lung complications in obese patients. Normal lung function depends on movement of the diaphragm up and down below the lung cavity on the one hand and free movement of the chest wall (rib cage) on the other. This way the lung, which contains a lot of elastic tissue, can expand actively by breathing in utilizing the breathing muscles and empty itself by the passive elastic forces within the lung tissue. There are two problems in the obese patient. First, the abdominal fat inside the abdominal cavity is like a roadblock against the diaphragmatic movements. This means the obese patient is much more reliant on active chest movements. Second, the rib cage has already been forced to be somewhat opened up, and active breathing movements will take more force to reach maximum possible lung capacity but will never be as good as in lean persons. This means that with any kind of exercise or stress, obese patients will have to breathe more rapidly to achieve the same air exchange. With chest infections the obese patient is at a higher risk for developing pneumonia, particularly in the lower parts of the lungs. From these lung regions, it is more difficult to cough up secretions, making the lower lung segments more prone to developing pneumonia. Sleep apnea is another potentially dangerous condition that is significantly more common in obese patients. The doctor may want to order sleep studies to monitor this.

Chapter 4:
The Food Factor

We are what we eat—a mixture of protein, fats, carbohydrates, supplemental vitamins, and minerals. I believe that the best diet is one that sticks close to the healthy dietary habits of those who live long, fulfilled lives and have lots of energy until a ripe old age. The population of Okinawa comes to mind (Willcox et al., 2001).

For balanced nutrition we need protein and essential fatty acids. Protein builds our cells, organs, and muscles and supplies us with essential amino acids, the building blocks for the peptide hormones in the brain and ACTH (the major stress hormone). Hormones are needed as communication signals between organ systems. Essential fatty acids, which are responsible for information transfer in our system, consist of omega-6 and omega-3 fatty acids, which cannot be made by our bodies. We must supply them to our body, and that is why they are called essential fatty acids.

Other building blocks are carbohydrates. In response to carbohydrate and sugar intake, the body releases insulin, the "storage hormone." It "files" the nutrients into the cells for future use. Unlike the amino acids and the fatty acids, there is not an essential carbohydrate, and yet we need carbohydrates as an energy source for all cell function. If no carbohydrates are forthcoming, the body is able to make glucose (the main carbohydrate) from protein or fat that is stored in the cells. Without carbohydrates our system would not be functioning smoothly.

Finally, our food has to supply us with vitamins and minerals. Both are found mixed in with animal protein sources as well as with carbohydrate sources, such as fruit and vegetables. This will be discussed in detail in chapter 8.

Let us now have a look at these main players. To make the best choices for a balanced food intake, it is important to know in which foods we can find these components.

Protein Foods

Good sources of protein include meat, fish, dairy products, or non-GMO soy products. A limited amount of protein can be found in legumes like dried beans, peas, or lentils. (As they do not contain all the essential amino acids, which are the building blocks of protein, they are also called "incomplete" proteins.)

Desirable protein foods are high in protein and low in fat. This includes lean cuts of beef and pork, chicken, and turkey (with the skin removed before cooking, as it is high in undesirable fats). Another good choice is fish or other seafood. Processed meats like hamburger are a second-class option. If you do eat them, be sure their fat content is 10 percent or lower, but stay away from processed meats, which contain too much salt, preservatives, fat, and even some recycled low-quality cut-offs. You will want to choose the lean variety only. The less costly "regular" ground beef has too much undesirable fat. Besides, you will likely drain and discard the fat when you cook it, so you'll wind up with less, meaning you have not saved money after all, but poured it down the drain! Cold sandwich meats are a questionable source of protein. Often they are high in fat and sodium, and many are processed with sodium nitrite or smoked (and thus contain cancer-producing substances).

> **Processed meats: A less desirable protein source, also source of poisonous sodium nitrite/nitrate**
>
> Ignore the hot dogs, wieners, sausage links, bologna, and salami. Not only are they high in fat, but they are also loaded with salt and sodium nitrite, or nitrate, a common preservative in the meat-processing industry. While sodium nitrate gives meat the appearance of freshness by enhancing its red color, it is a carcinogenic substance. Research has confirmed that it causes cancer of the esophagus, stomach, and bowel. You may think that small amounts can't hurt much, especially since it is permitted in food processing. You better think twice: many dangerous substances are used, and even if the knowledge is out that they are harmful, it takes a long time and often a lot of disease before the alarm goes off! You are the consumer: buyer beware! Look out for lean sandwich meats (chicken breast and turkey breast), and read the labels. If you are at the deli counter and you cannot see the labels, ask before you buy. Products without sodium nitrate are available.

Eggs are a good source of protein except that we have to monitor our yolk intake. You see, it is the egg white that we should use more liberally. The egg yolk contains a substance called arachidonic acid, which is metabolized in our liver into bad cholesterol (LDL). This can elevate cholesterol levels in our blood. We still can enjoy an omelet if we use only one egg and add two additional egg whites. Another possibility is to use egg white only, which is commercially available in the refrigerated section of your grocery store. (Buy the organic kind—it is by far the best quality.) Read the ingredients of egg substitute, if this is your choice, but know that it is less valuable than organic egg white.

Poisonous sodium nitrite/nitrate:

Esophageal cancer prevention: Have you checked your food labels lately? Look for nitrites and nitrates in sausages, ham, turkey breast, meats, and cheeses. You may have to ask your deli clerk to show you the label on the big package before he or she slices it for you. Many manufacturers are aware that nitrates and nitrites are mild carcinogenics. There is research that showed that nitrates and nitrites will chemically react with aminoacids from food to form nitrosamines in the stomach. These are cancer-producing chemicals, but the FDA never labeled them as such. Manufacturers often do not include nitrites or nitrates in the product label or it is labeled as curing salt in sausages and processed deli meats. Others are oblivious to the medical literature on this topic, possibly because of lobby groups. If you cannot find a brand that does not contain nitrites or nitrates, you are better off cooking your own meat and slicing it. Your health is at stake!

Source: Sears, B, 2001.

Protein from dairy products is best chosen from the lower-fat varieties: milk (2 percent), yogurt or cottage cheese (also available with 5 percent fat or less), and cheeses with a lower fat content (part-skim mozzarella can come in at a low 15 percent, and string cheese is similar). There are other varieties that are low in fat and tasty: ricotta (10 percent), provolone (24 percent), and cantenaar (18 percent), as well as the lighter versions of cheddar, swiss, and gouda. If in doubt, ask at the deli counter. If the fat percentage is higher, you have to automatically restrict the quantities you consume. Limit the high-fat varieties like cream cheese and the double-crème varieties of camembert or brie and mascarpone. While these are all sources of protein, the fat content has spiraled too high for your benefit! One word for consumers in the United States: bovine growth hormone is in your milk and milk products unless the product is organic. In Canada and European countries, bovine growth hormone is illegal, so it is not found in dairy products. One solution is to buy goat milk, goat cheeses, goat yogurt. Or buy organic milk and milk products if you insist on cow's milk. You will be pleased to find that cheeses from European producers are superior in quality, as a lot of them are made from milk that comes from grass-fed cattle.

Protein from soybeans has been consumed for centuries in Asia, mainly in China and Japan. It is an excellent choice for vegetarians. Tofu is the curd, which is derived from soy milk. It is available in two main varieties: soft (for desserts) and firm. Some varieties come baked in a tomato sauce or in a spicy teriyaki sauce. Tofu is a "chameleon" food: it is readily adaptable to various flavors. If you taste it without anything else added, you will probably find it too bland to be enjoyable. So experiment by adding your favorite spices, sauces, and condiments. The isoflavones that occur in soy products have received a lot of positive press lately: flavonoids are useful to protect against cancer and heart disease. Soy milk can be used if a person cannot drink cow's milk. Products vary greatly. Some are quite high in carbohydrates, which is usually due to the addition of sugar. When you read the ingredients on the package, this is quite obvious. Also, the calorie content will be a whopping 150 calories per cup, as compared to milk, which has no more than 100 calories. Look for a product that is comparable to milk. Remember, you are looking for a source of protein—not for extra sugar! Lately there is one big concern: more and more soy protein is derived from genetically modified soybeans. Until the long-term scientific studies are out, I would not take the risk: stay away from soy that is not organic or that could be genetically modified, as this has been associated with autoimmune diseases and may cause infertility in humans. A good source of protein without the problems of genetic modifications or bovine growth hormone contamination are organic meats and goat dairy products.

Another vegetable protein, also derived from soy, can be found in the Indonesian product tempeh. It is less commonly available, but Asian markets will carry it in the refrigerated or freezer section. It's best to buy organic tempeh to bypass possible GMO contamination.

Finally a growing number of soy products have turned up in the refrigerated or frozen section of our food markets: soy patties, burgers, hot dogs, sandwich slices, and varieties that mimic chicken burgers and nuggets except that they are made of soy and are not deep fried. None of those products can be trusted unless all the ingredients are organic. Most of them are not! In the United States and Canada, there is no mandatory lableling of GMO soy, and this makes me stay away rather than risk eating it. And no matter which way you look at all the soy dogs, soy patties, and soy bacon, they are all highly processed, which I consider more fake than food.

Let us look at another important member of the nutrition team.

The fat factor

Fat has been approached with caution, and it has often been perceived as the villain, the enemy responsible for obesity, heart disease, clogged arteries, and other ailments. A lot of products that line the supermarket shelves proudly proclaim they are "no-fat" or "low-fat" or "cholesterol-free." First of all, it is necessary to realize that some fats are essential and vital for us. As mentioned before, the body cannot make essential fatty acids out of other nutrients, so we need to supply them. In addition, a small amount of fat in our food helps to slow down the entry of carbohydrates into the bloodstream. It also sends signals to the brain so that we feel satiated and no longer hungry. As a sensible rule of thumb, we should not exceed 30 percent of our caloric intake from fat.

A group of "good" fats are the monounsaturated fats. They occur in olives or olive oil, avocados, almonds, and macadamia nuts.

Next are the polyunsaturated fats, which are divided into two groups. First are those containing omega-3 fatty acids, a healthy fat source occurring in foods like salmon, mackerel, sardines, tuna, or fish oil. Second is the subgroup containing omega-6 fatty acids, including corn oil, sesame oil, and grape-seed oil. These fats need to be balanced by omega-3 fatty acids; otherwise, they could lead to inflammatory conditions like arthritis (Sears, B, 2001, page 262).

It is the saturated fats that were considered to be the "bad" fats. They occur in animal fats like butter, lard, and dairy fat, but they are also found in tropical oils (palm oil or coconut oil). There has been a 180 degree turnaround as indicated in more recent work (Davis, 2011 and Perlmutter, 2013). Saturated fats are now considered to be neutral and even helpful to suppress your appetite for unhealthy sugars and starches.

Unfortunately there is another group that is the worst of them all, those fats that contain trans fatty acids. They are called *trans fats* and are the new bad kid on the block: before the twentieth century, they did not exist. They were developed in an effort to transform liquid oils into a spreadable fat. Also, the shelf life of products containing trans fats is longer. This way, butter—an animal fat that forms the bad cholesterol, plugs up arteries, and leads to heart attacks and strokes—was replaced, and margarine was created. It certainly was cheaper than the expensive butter; also it did not turn rancid like butter. But the trans fats in margarine are even worse than the fat in butter. Trans fats raise the bad cholesterol and at the same time lower the good cholesterol, which is a double whammy to wreak havoc with our health! Despite all the claims that some margarines are lower in trans fat than others and labels like "heart healthy," beware! Trans fats can be disguised on food labels as ""hydrogenated"; this means "bad trans fats"! Foods with high trans fat levels are best avoided altogether: deep-fried foods like french fries, chips, or nachos are on this list. Cookies, pies, and snack foods are also on the list, and so are commercial bakery products prepared with shortening. The harmless-sounding term *pure vegetable shortening* refers to a trans fat and is not harmless at all!

FAT: THE GOOD, THE BAD, AND THE UGLY

TYPE OF FAT		COMMENTS
Good	Omega-3 fatty acids	• the only essential fatty acid the body cannot make • found in salmon, mackerel, sardines, tuna, and fish oil
	Monounsaturated fatty acids	• not prone to oxidizing • no effect on insulin • found in olives, olive oil, avocados, almonds, and macadamia nuts
Neutral	Omega-6 fatty acids	• only neutral if balanced with omega-3 fatty acids • found in corn oil, sesame oil, and grape-seed oil
Bad in the past, now neutral	Saturated fats	• raises LDL cholesterol • found in butter, lard, dairy fat, and tropical oils (palm oil and coconut oil)
Ugly	Hydrogenated fat or partially hydrogenated fat, trans fatty acids, pure vegetable shortening	• good for long shelf life of cookies, bad for your heart • increases LDL and lowers HDL • found in margarine, deep-fried foods, and vegetable shortening

Source: Willcox et al., 2001 (p. 108-109, modified)

For the past 30 years we have been told that a high carb/low fat diet would be required to keep our arteries healthy and prevent heart attacks and strokes. The thinking was that fat in the arteries was what causes blockage, so perhaps one should cut out fats to prevent this from happening.

Read more info about it in the Wheat Belly diet book (Davis, 2012).

Saturated fats were thought to be bad for us, but newer research points to the fact that it is inflammation that is the important part. We have consumed too much sugar and starch that causes inflammation from too much insulin and causes oxidization of the LDL cholesterol, which in turn leads to fat deposits in the arteries (Schmid, 2013).

The "lipid theory of the development of cardiovascular disease" was very popular in the seventies and eighties, largely because sponsors of the vegetable-oil industry and the margarine industry had been lobbying influential regulatory bodies, such as the FDA. At a consensus conference in 1984, so-called experts (i.e., key marketing personnel) formulated strong guidelines about what a normal cholesterol level should be and how this should be achieved with a special cholesterol-lowering diet. If you want to read the full story about this incredible distortion of the truth, visit the website under the references ("Know your fats; the oiling of America").

A few years later, clinical guidelines for treatment with statin drugs were added (you guessed right, sponsored by Big Pharma). But hard scientific evidence did not confirm the lipid theory that saturated fats would cause hardening of the arteries or the claim that statin drugs would prevent deadly strokes and heart attacks. In fact, the opposite was shown to be true: saturated fat (meat, butter, cheese) and mono-unsaturated fat (olive oil, coconut oil) are neutral in terms of hardening of arteries. One's total cholesterol level can be well into the 200s and still be safe as long as the ratio of total cholesterol to HDL is less than 3.4. What has been found to be the culprit for hardening of the arteries is the consumption of sugar, starch, and wheat, which causes oxidation of LDL cholesterol. Trans fats do this as well. Ironically, overconsumption of these foods came as a result of the 1984 consensus, which recommended a low-fat and high-carbohydrate diet to prevent heart attacks and strokes. This diet has caused a vicious cycle: the pancreas overproduces insulin, and the liver changes carbohydrates into cholesterol and triglycerides, which are stored as fat in the body. The inflammation started by the change in metabolism is further worsened by inflammatory cytokines released from the fat that is hiding between the bowels (called "visceral fat"). Ultimately the cycle ends with the metabolic syndrome. As we know, the good news is that if you change your diet back to the old-fashioned diet that fitted our metabolism for millions of years—consisting of few carbs and medium to high amounts of saturated fats—the insulin response will stop, the fat will gradually melt away, and some of the atheromatous plaques in the arterial walls can disappear, reversing the situation (Schmid, 2013).

To summarize the fat story, I would like to leave you with some practical guidelines for shopping and food preparation:

The dos and don'ts about fat intake

To make sensible and healthy choices, you do not need a degree in nutrition. All you have to do is this:

1. Read labels and ingredient lists.

2. Avoid products that contain hydrogenated or partially hydrogenated fats (these different sounding names are synonyms for trans fats)

3. Eat one food per day that contains omega-3 fats. (If you do not like fish, take two to three capsules of molecularly distilled fish oil every day.)

4. Use monounsaturated fats like olive oil and coconut oil.

5. Aim for fat content of 25% to 30% of your total calories per day. Cholesterol intake should be less than 200 mg per day. Do not exceed the 30% mark. This means that you will look for fat amounts of 18% to 24% in cheeses, 2% cottage cheese for snacking, and lower-fat yogurt (2% to 4%).

With these simple guidelines, fat will be your nutritional ally and not an enemy.

Here is a story of how omega-3 fatty acids influence our mood. It turns out that these essential fatty acids are important for normal brain-cell function (blog dated July 2003). According to this article by Dr. Susan Biali (practicing family physician with a degree in dietetics), there is good evidence in the medical literature to indicate that the concentration of a number of brain hormones depends on what we eat. The five major items she pointed out are summarized below.

BRAIN FOOD COMPONENTS THAT AFFECT YOUR MOOD

FOOD ITEM	COMMENTS
Omega-3 fatty acids	• Chinese and Taiwanese eat much more of these and have 10 times less depression than North Americans.
DHA, a long-chain omega-3 fatty acid	• Our daily intake is 100 mg less per day than 50 years ago due to our diet being based on commercial livestock. Lack of DHA leads to depression.
Omega-6 fatty acid (from processed foods)	• The ratio of omega-6 to omega-3 has increased from fast-food consumption; this causes arachidonic acid to increase and leads to depression.
Folate and Vitamin B12	• Deficiency of these vitamins is associated with depression.
Tryptophan	• This is an essential amino acid that is needed to make serotonin, a brain hormone without which we experience depression.

Extensive medical literature points out that these various food factors are vital to our having a balanced mood. When these ingredients are present, our mood is more likely to be normal and more resilient to depression. The literature centers on various population groups in comparison with the North American population. For instance, one study reported that Taiwanese and Chinese people consume a lot more foods rich in omega-3 fatty acids, such as fish, than North Americans. In the same study, the rate of major depression was found to be ten times more frequent in North Americans, and the investigators felt that this was so because of the hormone-stabilizing effect of the omega-3 fatty acids. In addition, chronic stress also leads to a breakdown of omega-3 fatty acids in the brain, which eventually results in depression. Several nutritional factors appear to have caused deficiency states of essential brain nutrients, one being junk foods like candy bars, french fries, and hamburgers, leading to a disbalance of the ratio between the omega-6 fatty acid to the omega-3 fatty acid in our food (University of Maryland: Omega-6 fatty acids). Another factor is the increase in consumption of highly refined carbohydrates (sugar and starch), also called high-glycemic foods. This is known to lead to the metabolic syndrome. Finally, many people still have too much fat in their diets due to a high amount of hydrogenated vegetable oils.

So what is "brain food"? Dr. Biali points out in her article that it is always best to start with a low-fat, well-balanced food plan in which processed foods are avoided and vegetables and fruit provide the low-to medium-GI carbohydrates. Fish should be eaten at least three times per week to provide the brain with the essential omega-3 fatty acids. If you eat enough protein (meat, soy protein, milk products), the body can pick and choose what it needs in terms of amino acids, including tryptophan. (In other words, no tryptophan supplementation is recommended.) With folates one needs to be careful not to exceed 0.8 mg per day as with megadoses of folate (in the 15 mg range) toxic symptoms of vivid dreams, disturbed sleep patterns, and even occasional seizures develop. A good multivitamin supplement will not only provide the right folate dose, but also vitamin B12, which is also needed to prevent depression and hardening of the arteries by lowering homocysteine levels (re. folate see August 2008 blog).

Carbohydrates

Carbohydrates come in a dazzling diversity of foods. There is one common denominator: all of them occur in food derived from plants. Carbohydrates are important to our physical function. But like any member of the nutrition team, they can be beneficial, or they can be a nutritional nightmare. Food can be a powerful drug, and ultimately we are the users responsible for the proper dosage. Carbohydrate foods can be high-density carbohydrates. This means that they are transformed into glucose and released into our bloodstream in a fairly rapid fashion. As a result, the release of insulin is also relatively fast: there is a fast high peak of insulin levels. However, there will be a fairly rapid drop in insulin levels after a few hours. The result is that we feel hungry and are ready for some more. The coffee break with a cookie or a muffin or the midafternoon slump comes to mind. To get more order into the confusing array of carbohydrates, the glycemic index has been developed. It describes the impact a certain carbohydrate food group has on the body.

Glycemic index

Let me clarify the glycemic index (GI) further, as it is important in understanding which foods we should seek and which foods we should avoid. The glycemic response is derived from the height of the blood sugar level that occurs when pure sugar is absorbed by the gut into the bloodstream. This level was established as the norm and is arbitrarily given a value of 100 percent. Any other carbohydrate, generally speaking, leads to a lesser response, as the sugar level after absorption is less. The following table lists the high-GI foods that you should avoid.

HIGH-GLYCEMIC FOODS (HIGH-GI FOODS) TO AVOID

FOOD	GI	FOOD	GI	FOOD	GI
doughnut	76	breakfast cereal: Cheerios, corn bran, cornflakes, Cream of Wheat, Grape-Nuts flakes, Crispix, Rice Krispies, Shredded wheat, Raisin bran	70–87	glucose	100
corn chips	74			honey	87
white rice	72			sucrose (table sugar)	75
watermelon	72			dates	100
Aunt Jemima waffles	76			cookies like vanilla wafers, graham wafers	76
white bagel	72	instant rice	80	maltose	105
white bread	70	tapioca with milk	81	white potato, mashed	70

Source: modified from Sears, 2000 (pages 99/100)

It is generally accepted that a low glycemic index is up to 55 percent, a medium index ranges from 56 to 70 percent, and a high index is above 70 percent. Low- and medium-GI foods are recommended; the high-GI foods should be avoided. The above table gives you a flavor of what to avoid. These are the foods that cause an insulin surge and keep on feeding into the reactive hypoglycemia response by stimulating the pancreas to produce another insulin response.

Now that you know which foods to avoid, what foods are recommended? They are the foods that will not cause the pancreas to produce an overabundance of insulin. So they would also be the foods that diabetics could eat. Below I have summarized them in a table: Low (<55%) and medium (55 to 70%) glycemic foods that are recommended.

For more detailed food lists with glycemic values, I recommend this site on the Internet: http://www.lowglycemicdiet.com/gifoodlist. html

RECOMMENDED LOW/MEDIUM GLYCEMIC FOODS

FOOD	GI	FOOD	GI	FOOD	GI
fructose	20	cherries	22	sweet potatoes	50
agave nectar (1tbsp.)	11	raisins	65	tomatoes	38
strawberry jam (1tbsp.)	51	strawber-ries	32	chickpeas	36
stevia and other artificial sweeteners	0–2	apple	38	legumes (beans, lentils, black beans)	29–36
bran muffin	60	orange	40	soybeans	15
brown rice	55	pears	45	yogurt (plain)	35
cheese tortellini	50	mango	55	whole milk	27
meat ravioli	39	kiwi	52	ice cream	37–61
whole- grain bread	40–50	grapefruit	26	macaroni and cheese	64
pumpernickel (1 slice)	41	green peas	51	green veg-etables (lettuce, spinach, Swiss chard, etc.)	0–15
pineapple	66	long grain, white	44	barley, pearled	25

The densest form of carbohydrates will be found in products like sugar or honey. Any food prepared with sugar (jams, fruit spreads, cakes, cookies, desserts) will be a high-density carbohydrate food. Dense carbohydrates are also found in grains. As a rule of thumb, the more processed a grain is, the higher it is in carbohydrate density. All flour products fall into this category, like bread, buns, pasta, and all the highly processed breakfast cereals. Rice is another. Barley and oats (as long as they are not processed into flour) and instant cereals contain more fiber, making the transformation into glucose some-what slower.

Medium-density carbohydrate foods include root vegetables like potatoes, yams, turnips, carrots, and squash. Most fruit would rate as medium density, except for varieties that are high in sugar, like bananas, mangoes, or papayas. Obviously they are at the higher limit of medium. Also, dried fruit undergo a change in the processing: water is removed through dehydration, and the result is an intensely sweet product and a high-density carbohydrate food. Unfortunately this is also the case for raisins (dried grapes), which need to be consumed in small quantities—not by the handful.

Most vegetables fall into the low-density category, as they all contain a lot of fiber and water. This includes leafy vegetables like salad greens and spinach, chard, cabbage varieties, onions, peppers, tomatoes, mushrooms, green beans, and sprouts, like bean sprouts, alfalfa, or mixed sprouts. They are a great source of carbohydrates because they are slowly transformed into glucose, and this way the response of insulin is less dramatic. As a result of this knowledge, we are best off avoiding some of the densest carbohydrates. It may sound like a highly unpopular proposition, but sugar should be looked at as a condiment and not as a food, and the same is true for honey (Sears, B., 2000, p. 99).

Caution, health-food shoppers, regarding brown sugar and honey

Even though some health-conscious individuals look at honey as "natural" and for this reason superior, they overlook the fact that they are dealing with a highly concentrated, dense carbohydrate. Spoon for spoon it has the same disadvantageous effects on your metabolism as white sugar! It leads to the syndrome of insulin resistance, and after years of sugar overconsumption, this can cause inflammatory conditions like arthritis, diabetes, high blood pressure, heart attacks, strokes, Alzheimer's disease, dementia, and cancer. You may have thought of these medical conditions as genetically caused. The truth is that genetic factors must be activated by epigenetic factors to become effective, and sugar is one of these powerful triggers.

Use the medium-density carbs with prudence. There is definitely nothing wrong with carrots, but we certainly would not ingest a pound of them. Nor should we start drinking carrot juice by the glassful. It simply is too much of a good thing. In addition the fiber has been eliminated from it, so absorption of the sugar and starch is swift, leading to an insulin response. Likewise, a few slices of potato can enhance our dinner, but transforming several potatoes into a mound of mashed potatoes equals an overdose, which no diner should be subjected to. Finally, fruit will enhance and complement our carbohydrates, but the same guidelines apply: an apple can be part of a great breakfast or snack, but a glass of apple juice (the equivalent of three apples) is another story! The same is true for other fruit juices.

When it comes to low-density carbohydrates, we can feel free to fill our plate with salad greens, broccoli, tomatoes, or mushrooms. The benefit is also a good dose of fiber and an abundance of vitamins and minerals (Wiki review of low carbohydrate diets).

Looking at all these points, it becomes obvious that knowing our foods and their effect on our metabolism is essential when it comes to producing a meal that is beneficial and at the same time enjoyable.

High-carb/low-fat diet versus low-carb/medium-high healthy fat diet

There has been a paradigm shift in the thinking about how hardening of the arteries occurs. Now it is known that an inflammatory process causes it: an overindulgence in sugar, starch, and wheat products causes the liver to produce lipids and cholesterol and leads to the "wheat belly" (Davis, 2011) and the "grain brain" (Perlmutter, 2013). All of this causes cytokines to bring about an inflammatory reaction that affects the lining of arteries, causing not only heart attacks and strokes, but also Parkinson's disease, MS, autism, asthma, arthritis, epilepsy, Lou Gehrig's disease and Alzheimer's disease (Perlmutter, 2013). The inflammation does not stop there. If you keep up the high-carb/low-fat diet, it will lead to various cancers (Davis, 2012 and Perlmutter, 2013). The solution is a diet high in healthy fats as outlined above, with 20 percent protein, 50 percent complex carbs, and none of the refined carbs. I have followed such a diet since 2001. I am happy that I can now eat a reasonable amount of healthy fats, which I was not aware of being allowed before completing the research for this book. I continue with the antioxidant vitamins and anti-inflammatory supplements to prevent LDL oxidization. I hope that many of you can benefit from prevention so you can enjoy a healthy life without being a victim of illness or disability.

The idea of "the daily bread" is deeply ingrained in our culture. If you are like most people, you probably still think that so-called healthy grains like wheat are good for you and are "essential for a well-balanced diet." Ever since Kellogg's introduced cereal for breakfast and the bagel was invented as a midmorning snack, the agro industry and the food industry have lobbied to make grains prominent in the USDA food pyramid, which has recently been changed into the "choose your plate diet ("choose my plate" or "food pyramid" diet). Other agencies, including the Heart Foundation, the Academy of Nutrition and Dietetics (formerly "American Dietetic Association"), and the American Medical Association, have reiterated this statement about grains over and over until both the public and physicians accepted this as the truth. However, the scientific data does not support this point of view, it has been a myth!

We are gradually learning that a deliberate misinformation campaign has been going on since as far back as 1984 (and even before). It was that year that a consensus panel came up with revised "normal" values for cholesterol, and we as the medical profession (myself included) were told to treat high cholesterol levels much earlier and more aggressively than in the past with statins. Big Pharma is still pushing for this method of treatment. Now that I have been retired for more than four years, I can freely write about what is really going on. The truth has already leaked out, but it is not yet common knowledge.

Below I will review the switch from the old school of thought that a high-carb/low-fat diet is healthy to the new school of thought that a low-carb/medium high healthy-fat diet is healthy. Before you panic, sit back, relax, and read what I am saying.

A brief history of the high-carb/low-fat diet recommendation

The Framingham Heart Study, ongoing since 1948, followed a large group of people for decades to sort out what causes heart attacks and strokes and how to develop a program of prevention. This objective at the beginning of the study was very noble and promising. However, as time went on, the results from the study that were published intermittently appeared more and more confusing.

First there was the observation that high lipids (called triglycerides) and high cholesterol in the blood would cause heart attacks and strokes. It was assumed that fats in the diet must have caused this. Based on this thinking, the lipid theory of arteriosclerosis was formulated, a theory trying to explain how heart attacks were caused (PubMed "lipid theory").

If this theory were true, a lowering of the blood lipids and cholesterol should have lowered the rates of heart attacks and strokes. Thus many large trials were done, and the statins were developed to lower cholesterol. In a recent blog, I have explained that this has not lowered the mortality rates from heart attacks and strokes (Nov. 2013 blog). But instead of admitting that the researchers made a mistake, many are still doggedly holding on to the dogma of the lipid theory. The truth is that the lipid theory has not been proven to be true; the recommendation of a high-carb/low-fat diet has also not saved lives by preventing heart attacks and strokes. In fact, the opposite is true: older people with high cholesterol live longer and have less Alzheimer's disease than those with lower cholesterol levels in the blood (Perlmutter, 2013).

Dr. Perlmutter mentioned a study from the Netherlands (Perlmutter, 2013 [page78]) that for ten years followed 724 individuals who on average were eighty-nine years old. Those with high cholesterol lived longer than those with low cholesterol, exactly the opposite of what the lipid theory predicted! Specifically, for each 39 percent increase in cholesterol, there was a 15 percent decrease in risk of mortality. Think about it: the brain and the heart have LDL receptors on their cell surfaces for a reason. The reason is that both vital organs burn fat and need cholesterol to build up the membranes of the brain and heart cells.

Despite this compelling evidence, Big Pharma is in denial, and you will still find the lipid theory of arteriosclerosis heavily mentioned on the Internet as the only "valid" explanation for how heart attacks and strokes are caused.

Inflammation as the alternative explanation of arteriosclerosis

In the midnineties the first reports surfaced to explain that about 50 percent of patients with normal cholesterol levels still develop heart attacks. In these patients the C-reactive protein, an inflammatory marker, was very high, indicating that an inflammatory process had likely caused their illness.

Subsequently further research was able to show that the LDL cholesterol, when oxidized by sugar, was responsible for clogged arteries in these patients. It also became apparent that diabetics have a much higher risk of developing heart attacks than patients with normal blood sugars. This led to the conclusion by several different research teams that the lipid theory was wrong and needed to be abandoned.

A new theory has developed that explains that heart attacks and strokes develop in patients in whom free radicals have damaged LDL cholesterol. This damaged, oxidized LDL cholesterol leads to hardening of the arteries (arteriosclerosis). Sugar from increased carbohydrate intake has a lot to do with this: it leads to glycation of protein, causing advanced glycation end products, or AGEs ("Other cause of wrinkles").

AGE is an appropriate abbreviation for these products, as they really are the cause of premature aging, wrinkles, premature hardening of arteries, and a fifty-fold risk of free radical formation. This in turn will lead to more tissue aging. LDL used to be thought of as the "bad" cholesterol; I myself used that term in the past. LDL is now known to be a friendly and important transport form of cholesterol; it is sent from the liver to the brain and heart cells that need it for their metabolism. If LDL is oxidized, however, it becomes useless, and the heart and brain cannot absorb cholesterol for membrane synthesis via the LDL receptors. The end result is that vital organs like the heart and the brain do not get enough oxygen and nutrients, which leads to heart attacks and strokes. The free radicals that are released from oxidized LDL cholesterol and that circulate in the blood cause an inflammatory response in the lining of the arteries all over the body, which you know as hardening of the arteries (arteriosclerosis).

This may sound complicated, but all you need to remember is that sugar and starch consumption lead to accelerated hardening of arteries in your body, which causes heart attacks and strokes.

Reassessment of what a heart-healthy, brain-friendly diet is

The above-mentioned research findings require a complete rethinking of what a healthy diet is. The villain turned out to not be saturated fat (meat, eggs, butter, and avocado), but rather trans fat (margarine, hydrogenated polyunsaturated fatty acids), and I agree with the FDA that trans fats should be abolished (Politico website). Trans fat is full of free radicals that oxidize LDL cholesterol, which we just learned is causing hardening of arteries. But other villans are sugar and starches as they also lead to oxidization of LDL with subsequent fat deposits in the arteries. Omega-6 fatty acids, found in safflower oil, sunflower oil, grape-seed oil, and canola oil, are bad for you also, as they lead to inflammation through the arachidonic acid system in the body ("Arachidonic Acid" website). Conversely flaxseed oil and omega-3 fatty acids (EPA and DHA) derived from fish oil are very protective (anti-inflammatory) oils, as are olive oil and coconut oil. These latter two are anti-inflammatory monounsaturated fatty acids. Keep in mind that you want to change the ratio of omega-3 to omega-6 fatty acids more in the direction of omega-3 fatty acids so that the ratio will be between 1:1 and 1:3. Most Americans are exposed to ratios of 1:8 to 1:16 (from omega-6 fatty acids in fast food and processed foods), which leads to inflammation of the arteries as well.

The new heart- and brain-healthy diet consists of no refined carbohydrates (sugar and starch), but about 50 percent complex carbohydrates (organic vegetables like broccoli, spinach, cauliflower, brussels sprouts, peppers, onions, garlic, peppers, swiss chard, zucchini, asparagus, and so on), 20 percent protein, and 30 percent saturated and other fats like omega-3 (1:3 mix with omega-6) fatty acids and monounsaturated fats (like olive oil or coconut oil).

You can even eat butter, lard, and other animal fats, provided they come from clean animals that haven't been treated with antibiotics or bovine growth hormone (Davis, 2012). Even extreme diets like the Inuit diet (with 80 percent saturated fat and 20 percent protein) lead to longevity with healthy arteries (Perlmutter, 2013). The patients who died in the many trials, including the Framingham Heart Study, did so because of free radicals from sugar, starch, and wheat. Wheat contains the addictive gliadin molecule (part of gluten), which makes people eat more sweets and starchy foods. The liver turns the extra calories into visceral fat deposits that in turn cause the release of cytokines like tumor necrosis factor alpha (TNF alpha) and COX-2 enzymes ("In depth report about hardening of arteries"). This causes inflammation, heart attacks, strokes, and cancer. Inflammation has also been dealt with by Dr. Frank Lipman's website "Natural Remedies For Inflammation".

Contrary to what Big Pharma wants you to know, cholesterol is an anti-inflammatory substance ("Cholesterol as an anti-inflammatory"), LDL is a cholesterol transporter (provided it is not oxidized), and HDL is

protective of hardening of the arteries as long as the ratio of total cholesterol to HDL cholesterol is less than 3.4 for males and 3.3 for females. This
is the risk ratio used by cardiologists to determine the risk of coronary
artery disease. The average risk of this ratio for Americans is 5.0 for males
and 4.4 for females. The ideal ratio to strive for is the 1/2 average risk ratio
of 3.4 or less for males and 3.3 or less for women (Schmid, K., 2013).

Paradigm shift in causation of heart attacks and strokes, but also of cancer and neurological diseases

As pointed out by Dr. Perlmutter, there has been a paradigm shift
in our thinking about what causes inflammation and what causes all
of the major diseases, including premature aging (Perlmutter, 2013).
Many physicians are not up-to-date in this new thinking even though
it has been in the medical literature since about 1995. In my colleagues'
defense, I'd like to say that they are busy people and do not always
have the time to do their continuing education. However, it is imperative that the public learn about this paradigm shift, as it affects literally
everyone. In my YouTube video on the home page of my website, Net
Health Book (www.nethealthbook.com) I talked about this new thinking in the summer of 2012 (youtube.com/watch?v=3X69pmVb3O8).
Now we are learning that there is an anti-inflammatory, cholesterol-
containing, medium healthy-fat diet containing no refined carbs but
ample complex carbs; it is a modified Zone diet (Sears, 2001) or a modified Mediterranean diet. At the same time, it is a weight-loss diet, as
cholesterol and fat in your diet stop the liver from producing lipids and
cholesterol and helps you to lose weight. Critics will say that it is too
good to be true, but I agree with Dr. Perlmutter and Dr. Davis, both of
whom have provided ample evidence that it is true. Just read these
two references (Davis, 2012 and Perlmutter, 2013), and try some of their
recipes. One word of caution, though. Keep your egg consumption
below two and a half eggs (with yolks) per week. If you require more
egg protein, simply add organic egg white (none of the egg subsitutes
that have unhealthy fillers). It is the egg yolk that contains omega-6
fatty acids and that stimulates the arachidonic acid pathway. This is an

important point for prostate cancer prevention in males and for breast cancer prevention in females.

Practical hints about a healthy diet

You have met the team players in your nutrition. The proper structure of the team is called a healthy diet. Before we look at a well-balanced breakfast, lunch, or dinner, a few simple rules that apply to any meal should be established. We need to come to terms with the quantities, but it is clearly not an option to walk around with food scales in our backpacks. It is not necessary, either: eye measure can be a big help, and we can look at the size of the palm of our hand.

Start with a serving of lean protein. A serving should not be larger than the palm of your hand (some people relate to the size of a deck of cards, which is OK, too.) This also applies to the thickness. The lean protein foods are organic meats like skinned chicken breast, turkey breast (also without skin), lean beef, organic tofu, egg white, fish, or cottage cheese.

Fill the other two-thirds of the plate with low-density carbohydrate foods. Our choice would be vegetables, salad greens, and mushrooms. The variety is large! Root vegetables (potatoes, turnips, parsnips, carrots) and starchy vegetables like squash should be used sparingly. High-density carbohydrate foods like pasta, bread, buns, crackers, or rice should be avoided.

You do need a small portion of fat. Fat can come from two teaspoons of olive oil, or you can add six olives, two teaspoons of slivered almonds, a slice of avocado, or a few macadamia nuts.

Complete the meal with a piece of fruit. Fruit choices are abundant: try one cup of strawberries, a small orange, an apple, or one-fourth of a cantaloupe. You will want to restrict the intake of very sweet fruit varieties like papaya, pineapple, mango, or banana. Dried fruit should not be considered a fruit portion, as it is very high in sugar. It is best treated like a condiment.

This approach will leave you with a filled plate and a full stomach. What is even better is that this type of meal will keep you energetic and without any hunger pangs for four to five hours. When you review this model, notice that we are dealing with a wide variety of foods with lots of flavor and texture. It is also perfectly "real" food: no special diet products are needed. All of it is readily available at your regular supermarket. Finally, take note that highly processed foods and sugar-laden products are *not* part of the list.

You might wonder, "Now what's wrong with a breakfast of orange juice, a bowl of cornflakes in milk, and a coffee?" If you take a closer look, it becomes clear that you are getting a lot of high-density carbohydrates (in the cornflakes) and a significant amount of sugar (in the orange juice). The amount of protein in the milk is disproportionately small, and beneficial fats are missing. The result: three hours later—or even earlier—you will be as hungry as before. You'll find that your mental focus is poor, too, and you'll reach for—you guessed it—another source of sugar and starches, probably a muffin. The reason is simple: your blood sugar levels have dropped to a low, and your insulin levels are high, as you did not get the protein and fat you needed. Your meal was too high in dense carbs. Fine, you say. Let's try this one: "I'll have a plate full of scrambled eggs and bacon. Never mind the toast, and I'll skip the cereal, too." Again you will experience significant hunger after a few hours due to a meal that is solely focused on protein and fat. And bacon is not the most desirable fat source, not to mention the additives like sodium nitrates. You have skipped any carbohydrate source. There is no fiber that would bulk up the meal and keep you full for longer. Your intestines would love some vegetables like leafy greens. The minerals contained in the vegetables would also be an additional benefit to your body. So you see, it is all about the balance of carbohydrates, protein, and fat that keeps your system running smoothly.

Contrary to this, if you eat a meal that provides a balance of carbohydrates, protein, and fat, you will not be subject to hunger pangs and cravings after just a few hours. Also, your mental focus will stay clear, and your energy levels will be much increased. Besides balanced nutrition, it is crucial to your well-being that your body gets enough fluids. Keep in mind that 70 percent of your body is water. You excrete water through breathing, sweating, and eliminating urine and feces. Only you can replace the water. Drink spring water or other purified water. You will want to avoid chlorinated water, if only for the reason that it does not taste good! You'll probably drink more in a warmer climate, but two liters (67.6 fluid ounces) is a good daily intake. Carry a water bottle when you are on the go.

A model for a healthy, nutritional day

Breakfast: ⅔ cup of rolled oats mixed with 1 small grated apple and 8 ounces (250 ml) of milk or soy milk. Add ½ scoop of protein powder, and top with 2 teaspoons of slivered almonds. Coffee, tea, herb tea, or water.

Lunch: 3½ ounces (100 g) of roasted chicken breast (or sliced turkey breast roast), 2 cups of romaine lettuce, and 1 sliced tomato with balsamic vinaigrette with 2 teaspoons of olive oil. For dessert: ¼ cantaloupe.

Afternoon snack: 4 ounces (125 ml) unsweetened yogurt with 4 chopped-up large macadamia nuts and ½ cup of grapes.

Dinner: Stir-fry with 2 cups of bean sprouts, 4 green onions, 1 cup sliced mushrooms and ½ green or red pepper. Use 2 teaspoons of olive oil for stir-frying, and add 4 ounces (110 g) of salmon pieces. Season with ginger and soy sauce. For dessert: 1 mandarin orange.

Late-night snack: ½ cup cheese and ½ orange cut into chunks with 4 slivered almonds sprinkled on top.

Another snack you may enjoy instead of the late-night snack could be 3 ounces wine and 1 ounce of cheese. Or enjoy 2 squares of dark chocoate (over 70% cocoa content).

These healthy eating habits are not flashy or glamorous; in fact, they're rather plain and a tad old-fashioned. When you visited with your favorite aunt or your grandmother, she might have told you the same.

Without going into the complex biochemistry of nutrients, a model for one day will follow. There is room for three meals and two snacks.

With this type of meal structure, you will not feel deprived or on edge; with properly balanced food intake, hunger pangs will become a thing of the past. You will, however, enjoy the benefits of feeling more energetic and very likely get rid of the midmorning carbohydrate cravings and the midafternoon slump.

Even with a busy schedule, good eating habits can be part of your day, and they should! You need the energy to get through the day. One approach that is easy and certainly very economical is packing your lunch and bringing it to work. But due to busy schedules and time constraints, we consume a high proportion of our meals in restaurants.

Eating out

Fast-food restaurants often come under fire and are blamed for poor nutrition. If you are an uninformed consumer, this will be true. Fast-food places can offer the good, the bad, and the ugly, and it's up to you to make the adequate nutritional choices as opposed to picking the quick, nonnutritional fix. Here is the URL of a site on the Internet that lists a number of good meal suggestions that are well balanced: http://www.100daysofrealfood.com/real-food-defined-a-k-a-the-rules/

Let's take the common scenario of lunch at a hamburger place. This table tells you what to look out for.

This type of selection fulfills the following criteria:

- having a protein portion (about the size of the palm of your hand)
- having carbohydrates (a salad, as well as the fruit)
- having a moderate amount of fat

Eating out: Lunch

1. Choose the grilled chicken item. Do not order the chicken burger, hamburger, or chicken nuggets.

2. Order your grilled chicken without mayonnaise, and forget the bun!

3. Order a side salad, and ask for dressing on the side—not poured over it. Use only part of the dressing.

4. Have a piece of fruit for dessert. You can bring an apple or buy one at the corner store.

Dinner, too, is frequently eaten in restaurants. The next table provides a sensible suggestion for this meal.

Eating out: Dinner

1. Study the menu, and pick a protein food that is lean. Look for nonbreaded fish or meat, or choose tofu if you are in an Asian restaurant.

2. Order a salad. Skip the croutons, and order the low-fat dressing on the side.

3. At the time of your order, request an extra side vegetable instead of the pasta, rice, or potatoes.

4. Forget the garlic bread or the dinner buns with butter.

5. Once your meal arrives, eat only the meat portion you need (remember the palm of your hand measure). Ask for a doggie bag for the surplus. You will enjoy it the next day.

6. Skip dessert unless it is a piece of fruit.

Even though you likely eat breakfast at home, things will be different when you are traveling.

If you are on the run and it is getting late, it is better to have a snack as a touch-up. Consider an apple or a mandarin orange, a piece of mozzarella (string cheese), or half a handful of almonds to tide you over till the next larger meal. Another option is to carry a nutrition bar in your pocket. Look for a product with a good balance of carbohydrates, protein, and fat. Some power bars do not offer you balanced ingredients: either they are too high in carbohydrates, or they overemphasize the amount of protein. Choose a bar with organic ingredients. While it's not your best choice, it's better than a bag of snack foods, chips, crackers, or other nonnutritional waste products that are peddled as snacks.

Eating out: Breakfast

1. Forgo the pancakes with syrup and the hash browns.

2. If there is a breakfast bar, have a small helping of oatmeal, eat a portion of scrambled eggs, and enjoy some fruit. This may be a little higher in fat than your usual breakfast.

3. Some restaurants will offer "heart smart" choices like an omelet made with either egg substitute or more egg whites than egg yolk. This would be a good choice, along with some fruit.

4. Drink tea or coffee with no sugar, or add sugar substitutes like stevia (comes in powder form or as prepackaged mini paper bags). Some cream is OK.

5. Remember, do not eat bread, toast, or ordinary cereal flakes, as these turn to pure sugar in your system within half an hour, starting the hyperinsulinism cycle and promoting the syndrome of insulin resistance (metabolic syndrome).

Shopping for the right foods

In order to prepare meals that look and taste great, you have to do your own shopping. Our supermarkets are like the land of plenty, but the overwhelming selection can make your shopping trip a confusing and tiring experience. Often the sigh of "I hate grocery shopping" expresses the feelings of the person who embarks on a shopping expedition. It can be a jungle out there.

With these points in mind and a list in your hand, a shopping expedition does not have to feel like a jungle trek. For the most part, you do not have to venture deep into the jungle: it is a good rule of thumb that most of your shopping is done at the periphery of the store. This is the area of fresh items, which you will peruse most of the time.

How to grocery shop

- Careful planning is the first step to a trek in the jungle!

- Have a list in a prominent place in your workshop. (Yes, your kitchen is exactly that!) Put items on your list when you notice that you are running out of them. Shopping with a list helps to put a lid on impulse buying and the well-known frustration of returning from a shopping trip and having forgotten an important item.

- Do your shopping when you are not hungry. It may sound funny, but market researchers noticed a long time ago that a lot of items look good to the shopper who is prowling the aisles at lunch or dinnertime and has an open stomach for food demos.

- Be wary of displays close to the checkout. They were placed there to entice you to buy while you are waiting in line, but a bargain you don't need is not really a bargain.

- Get to know the store and the products offered. Also know the prices.

Let's start at the deli. Your low-fat cheese varieties, roasted chicken, turkey breast, or lean ham, if you choose, are all found here.

Go on to the meats. Lean cuts of grass-fed beef, pork, chicken, and lamb will be found here.

Next, fish and seafood. Salmon, sole, cod, halibut, trout, mussels, and shrimp will be there to choose from. Limit seafood to once or twice per week. Be aware of contamination with heavy metals. Here is a website that deals with this and helps you to decide what type of seafood to buy: Natural Resources Defense Council website: http://www.nrdc.org/health/effects/mercury/guide.asp

Continue at the vegetarian section. Tofu or tempeh will be here. Look only for produce with the label "organic, non-GMO." Soy is almost 100 percent GMO in the United States and Canada.

Now the dairy section. Here you will find milk or soy milk, yogurt, cottage cheese, and more lower-fat cheeses (no cheese over 30 percent fat content). In the United States, bovine growth hormone is used to increase milk producion in cattle, but this substance is banned in Europe and Canada. I buy Canadian or European import cheeses, local goat milk and goat-milk cheeses (no bovine growth hormone contamination) when I travel in the United States. Generally every major supermarket in the United States and Canada sells organic cow's milk.

The bakery section. This section is also found at the periphery, but you will want to be very discerning, as these products don't offer much more than dense carbohydrates, trans fats, and a lack of minerals. The dozen bagels will not give you much nutritional bang for your buck. Don't waste your money! I walk by this section.

Finally you will arrive at the produce department. Look for the organic subsection. You will likely go for all the green-leaf choices, like leaf lettuce, kale, chard, and spinach, as well as the cabbage varieties (broccoli, green cabbage, sue choi, napa cabbage, and cauliflower). The other ones for your list are the intensely colored nonroot vegetables like tomatoes, red and green peppers, and mushrooms, which are a powerhouse of minerals, and green beans, asparagus, onions, and garlic. You will also buy your fruit: apples, oranges, grapefruit and other citrus, pears, and berries. Organic produce is safest to avoid pesticide contamination. I spend the extra dollar. Go easy on mango, papaya, and banana because of their high sugar content. An additional concern is that Hawaian papaya is 90 percent GMO! Here is a website that helps you to navigate through pesticide residues and GMO contamination: Environmental Working Group: http://www.ewg.org/enviroblog/2014/02/case-organic-over-conventional-fruits-and-veggies

The deep-frozen section can be your best ally. Look for deep-frozen vegetables, fruit, and fish, as well as meats. Because vegetables are quickly readied for the freezer, their vitamin content can actually be higher than that of a vegetable that has spent eight days in transit from the field to the produce department. The deep-frozen section also gives you access to variety. You'll be able to enjoy strawberries even when they are not in season. Read the labels, as some fruits have been packaged with sugar syrup. Look for the varieties with no added sugar. The frozen section also contains some highly processed items: deep-fried foods and dessert selections that are not contributing to your health, but rather only empty your wallet. Again, be wary of pesticide residues and GMO crops.

On the shelves you'll find canned foods. These can be useful as long as you are dealing with fruits canned in their own juices and not in sugar syrup. But canned fruits and vegetables contain fewer vitamins than their deep-frozen counterparts. And watch out for vegetable varieties with less salt added. The label will read "low sodium." I prefer fresh or deep-frozen fruit and vegetables.

You will not have to navigate all the aisles, only those that hold your cleaning products and cosmetics. You will also require some staples from the shelves: olive oil, olives, and almonds or macadamia nuts (these should be raw or dry roasted and unsalted). The one valuable cereal products will be coarse rolled oats, steel-cut oats, and some pot barley. Quinoa can be used as a grain, as it offers the highest protein content, but you should consume it in small quantities. Avoid the quick-cooking or instant oats.

Due to the processing, the carbohydrates in these products are absorbed a lot faster and consequently trigger a higher insulin response.

You might wonder about drinks next. Having passed the colas, ginger ales, and other sugar pops, you may eye the diet drinks. Beware of drinks sweetened with aspartame. There is increasing evidence that phenylalanine (aspartame, NutraSweet, or Sweet'N Low) is not a harmless sweetener. Newer research has shown that it can cause gastroesophageal reflux (GERD) and migraine headaches. Do not use Splenda (sucralose), a polymerized sugar product that was originally developed as an insecticide.

I did an experiment in Hawaii in which I poured a sample of Splenda onto ants. They first disliked it and avoided it. Later they tasted some of it. Twenty-four hours later, I found the shriveled bodies of hundreds of ants in the area where I had sprinkled Splenda! Since that experience, I have avoided the use of Splenda and anything prepared with sucralose. "So which sweetener is safe to consume?" Stevia, a sweetener from a South American plant, does not have harmful effects. Several good brand-names exist: KAL, Sweet Leaf, etc., but only tiny dosages are required.

You are best served with mineral water, purified drinking water, herbal teas, tea or coffee. Fruit juices do have vitamins and minerals, but they are high in sugar. You would not eat three large apples in one sitting, so why insist on drinking eight ounces of apple juice? You'll ingest all the sugar and forgo the fiber! You'll also notice that a lot of fruit juices have been mixed with sugar, water, artificial flavor, and some color. As an apology some vitamin C has been added, and so they are labeled as "a good source of vitamin C." In reality we are dealing with flavored, colored sugar water. You can decide whether you want to spend your dollars on this selection! I walk past without buying anything.

In the aisle adjacent to the pop, you will encounter a huge selection of convenience and snack foods. You have likely met them on TV. Some will be high in starches and fat (chips); others will be high in starches, sugar, and fat (cookies, donuts, cream pastries), All of them contain trans fats and/or omega-6 fats. Take some time to read the ingredients, and then decide whether you and those who eat in your household deserve nutritional garbage.

You have now completed your round trip in the supermarket.

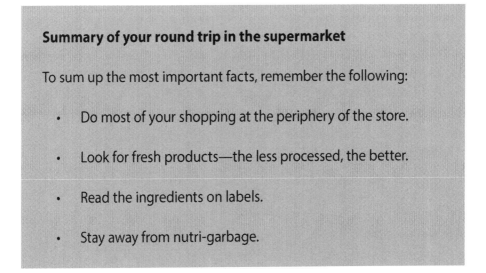

Summary of your round trip in the supermarket

To sum up the most important facts, remember the following:

- Do most of your shopping at the periphery of the store.

- Look for fresh products—the less processed, the better.

- Read the ingredients on labels.

- Stay away from nutri-garbage.

Food safety

Another important point once shopping is done is knowing how to store and handle food safely. All products that require refrigeration have to be kept cold and should be brought home to be stored in the refrigerator at 4°C (39.2°F). Deep-frozen foods have to be brought home and stored in the freezer at -18°C (0°F). Previously frozen or defrosted items cannot be refrozen!

I have a plug-in cooler in the car that keeps deep-frozen and refrigerated foods cold during the ride home and is also useful on longer trips when we stay in motels or hotels that have only a refrigerator in the room. If you don't have a portable freezer, in warmer weather you may need to carry a cold pack and an insulated bag. This is not an exaggeration. The critical time limit is two hours. Once this limit is exceeded, bacterial growth and spoilage result. Keeping a package of deli meats in a warm car during a daylong shopping trip translates very quickly into food-borne illness, or food poisoning. Bacteria and bacterial toxins are odorless and cannot be tasted, yet they can be extremely dangerous.

In the food preparation area, be meticulous about cleaning and sanitizing cutting areas that have been in contact with meat. Wooden cutting boards are inferior to nonporous cutting surfaces, which can be cleaned a lot more effectively with bleach and water.

All meats should be cooked until they are no longer pink, and special care has to be taken with ground meats. Once meat has been cooked, it has to be kept hot until consumption; if it was prepared ahead of time, it must be cooled down quickly and refrigerated. Never leave perishable foods like meat, eggs, cheese, or cooked meals at room temperature. Bacteria love room temperature and will multiply rapidly, and serious food-borne illness can be a consequence. So-called hamburger disease is not just an inconvenience with frequent bathroom visits. It can kill. The same goes for preparations containing egg, like mayonnaise, egg salads, salads with mayo-based dressings, or desserts made with egg whites. Keep them cold! Getting sick after a picnic is no joke. The culprit would be most likely the bacterium salmonella or E. coli, which, given a chance to multiply, can land you in the hospital.

It is also important to realize that vegetables that have residues of earth can be hazardous as well, as they can be a source of botulism, a highly dangerous form of food-borne illness. Never infuse garlic in oil and let it sit around at room temperature on your kitchen counter— this can be a culture medium for botulism spores! Keep it refrigerated, and discard it after one week.

These simple rules will prevent trouble.

> **A few basic food-safety rules**
>
> 1. Keep hot foods hot (65°C or 150°F, or over).
>
> 2. Keep cold foods cold (fridge temperature of 4°C or 39.2°F).
>
> 3. Clean and sanitize the surfaces where food is cut and prepared.
>
> 4. Observe good personal hygiene when you work with food. (Wash your hands!)

Chapter 5:
The Exercise Factor

Fitness has become a buzzword, and a whole industry has developed around it. It is time to demystify some of the points and questions that arise with an exercise program. For more details see the table below.

THE PLAIN TRUTH ABOUT FITNESS

COMMON CONCERNS	TRANSLATION INTO TRUTH
I cannot afford fitness gear.	You don't need special clothes. You probably have shorts and a T-shirt.
What about shoes?	All you need is a good pair of walking shoes or cross-trainers with proper arch support.

Can I start now?	**Absolutely! The only exception: if you have been chronically inactive or you have health problems, check with your doctor first.**
I have arthritis and joint pains.	**Swimming will be your best option. Check with your doctor if you have any doubts.**
Exercise is too difficult, as I'm overweight!	**It is not! Try swimming to get started.**
I get very sweaty and hot when I exercise. What can I do?	**Carry a water bottle. You need to replenish fluids. If you are in a warm climate, use common sense: to exercise early in the morning is best! Alternatively, exercise in an air-conditioned gym.**

Snacks and fitness

Fluid intake is crucial in any climate. Even when you are skiing in cold weather conditions, you lose fluids through perspiration and breathing. Carry your water! This brings us to the point of sports drinks. They contain sugar (for energy) and salt (to retain moisture). The truth is that you can do without salt (unless you embark on an expedition into the Mojave Desert).

You are also not served well with sugar as the quick fix, which does not do a good job for your overall performance. You are a lot better off having a small, nutritionally balanced snack consisting of carbohydrates, protein, and fat for your energy demands. A small apple, a piece of cheese, and half a dozen almonds will be a good touch-up. A nutrition bar with well-balanced ingredients will do the job, too. Besides eating the snack, do drink your water!

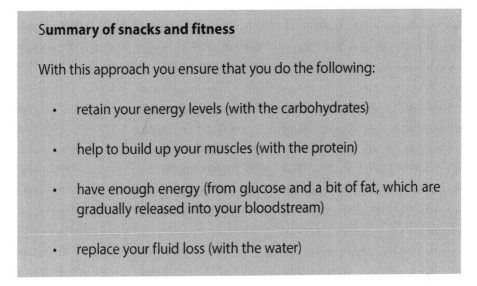

Summary of snacks and fitness

With this approach you ensure that you do the following:

- retain your energy levels (with the carbohydrates)

- help to build up your muscles (with the protein)

- have enough energy (from glucose and a bit of fat, which are gradually released into your bloodstream)

- replace your fluid loss (with the water)

If exercise is already part of your daily activities, the next points may not be big news to you. The benefit of physical activity lies in the regularity and the successful integration of it into our daily schedule. If we do not exercise on a regular, ongoing basis, we forgo many of the health benefits. Any athlete will be able to tell you a story about loss of muscle strength and endurance after an injury or illness. It takes a while to build muscle strength and endurance to the previous level after not having used those muscles for a few days or, worse, a few weeks!

The right dose of exercise

How much exercise do you need? Some researchers from Harvard came up with the following: the number of calories burned by exercise should be about 2,000 per week. Generally men will achieve that in a shorter time than women (assuming that males have more body weight and more muscle mass). About thirty minutes of power walking per day will be enough to burn 300 calories. A power walk is not a leisurely stroll: it's fast. It raises your heart rate, you may breathe a bit faster, and you'll work up a sweat. But it is easy to begin: all you need is a good pair of walking shoes. You can start at your front door, and you don't need to make a trip to the gym. You won't need special clothes or an exercise machine. For a number of people, walking with a partner or group is a lot more fun, so ask a friend or a neighbor. You may be surprised to find that a lot of people enjoy a brisk walk, and company keeps you motivated to stick to your program.

SOME COMMON EXERCISES TO CHOOSE FROM
Power walking
Treadmill exercise (a good alternative in bad weather)
Bicycling or riding a stationary exercise bike
Aerobic dancing, simple aerobics, Zumba, ballroom dancing
Jogging

There is simply no excuse for being unable to exercise, unless you are having severe health problems.

If you have a heart condition like angina or if you have suffered a heart attack, it is imperative that you discuss any fitness program with your doctor before you embark on it. There are specialized programs for people with a history of a heart attack, and they are very beneficial. Being very heavy is often perceived as a barrier to an exercise program, but remember that even whales are graceful in water. Go swimming! People who experience joint problems and pain due to arthritis as well as back pain sufferers will find swimming enjoyable, too. There is another positive aspect to exercise, whether it is aerobics or swimming. Certain brain hormones called endorphins are released. They are feel-good hormones: people experience a bit of a natural high and a sense of well-being through regular exercise. Pains and aches become less prominent. Already for this reason it is very desirable for a person with a condition like arthritis to stay active. You will soon discover which of the aerobic forms of physical activity works best for you. Whatever it is, build it into your day and make sure that those thirty minutes are enjoyable. If a snapshot of you exercising would depict exhaustion and acute suffering, you should probably review your exercise program. You may do more damage than good. It will also become increasingly difficult to put up with a source of distress, and after a while you'll be ready to throw in the towel. To avoid these pitfalls, gradually build up your endurance over a period of time.

Moderation succeeds, excess exercise causes harm

You may think that if thirty minutes of exercise are good, sixty minutes must be even better. But it does not work this way: with more intense exercise, the body has to cope with the demand. It is a stressful situation, and signals are sent to the brain accordingly: the stress hormone ACTH is released, stimulating the adrenal glands to secrete more cortisol. These elevated cortisol levels weaken the immune system and cause the body to age faster. In short, you may be a bit fitter, but you are accelerating the aging process, which is probably not the goal you had in mind.

The other equally important part of an exercise program is the anaerobic exercises

Anaerobic exercises are designed to strengthen your muscles. Weight lifting is one example of an anaerobic exercise. In a well-equipped gym, many options are available. There is one word of caution. Do not assume that you can start pumping iron like Superman. Start with low weights, and ask the fitness instructor for input. Stress cannot only be counterproductive; it can actually hurt or even kill you. It is usually type A personalities (who are driven) who get heart attacks with excessive exercise programs. So start low and go slow. Of

Modified push-ups in standing position

1. Stand in front of a wall (2 to 3 feet away).

2. Extend your hands in a straight line from your shoulders until they reach the wall.

3. Move your body toward the wall by bending your elbows, keeping the back straight. Then push away as you straighten your elbows until you return to the initial position.

4. Do a set of 10, pause for 1 minute, and repeat twice.

Here is a video showing this:

http://www.youtube.com/watch?v=1RtM3L00BUU

course, you do not need access to a gym to do muscle-strengthening exercises. You can acquire a set of dumbbells (three- to five-pound weights would be good for starting). For upper body strength training, push-ups work well. For the lower part of your body, knee bends (squats) are OK.

The following is a brief outline for upper body strength training. You may find the beginning disappointing, and the very word *push-up* may conjure up images of boot camp and torture. There is no need for torture: you can start out with a modified version.

Once this modified push-up exercise is easy, move on to a modification in which you use a table or a kitchen counter.

This is the example for the next modification:

Upper-body push-ups using table or counter

1. Stand in front of a table or the kitchen counter (2 to 3 feet away).

2. Extend your hands in a straight line from the shoulder to reach the tabletop. Keep your back straight, and lower your upper body to the tabletop by bending your elbows. Your shoulders will be over your hands.

3. Raise your upper body again by straightening the elbows, pushing back until you reach the initial position.

4. Repeat this exercise 10 times, pause for 1 minute, and do another 2 sets of 10 with a one-minute pause between sets.

Here is a video showing this:

https://www.youtube.com/watch?v=bcaHnXoc_ac

https://www.youtube.com/watch?v=bcaHnXoc_acOnce you can easily manage this push-up variation, you will be ready for the next variation, which starts from a kneeling position.

Once you have become comfortable with these modified push-ups, you can go on to the real mean push-ups, where only your toes touch the ground, your arms are fully extended, and your back stays straight. Again, three sets of ten push-ups with a one-minute pause between sets should do.

Upper-body push-ups in kneeling position

1. Kneel on the floor. (Note: people with arthritis in the knees or meniscal problems are exempt from this exercise.)

2. Extend your arms to the floor (as before in a straight line from the shoulder).

3. Lower yourself until first your hands touch the floor, at which time you should bend your elbows. Continue to lower your upper body until your chest touches the floor. (Don't drag your stomach on the floor!) Push yourself back to the initial kneeling position.

Do 3 sets of 10 push-ups with a 1-minute pause between sets.

Watch this video:

http://www.youtube.com/watch?v=49NR8BmQNcQ

P.S. If you still hate regular push-ups, stick to the modification that you can live with, or alternate between the various options.

Examples for lower-body strength training follow:

As was briefly mentioned before, a good basic exercise is the squat (also called a deep knee bend). Depending on your initial level of fitness, you may need to start slowly and use a chair with armrests for support.

Squatting exercise (deep knee bend)

1. Stand in front of a chair with armrests.

2. Place your hands on the armrests. Slowly lower yourself to the seat by bending your knees.

3. Raise yourself back up to the initial standing position.

Do a set of 10 squats, pause for 1 minute, and do 2 more sets of 10 squats with a 1-minute pause in between.

Watch this video for details (once you are comfortable without the support of a chair):

http://www.youtube.com/watch?v=E5li-45RiNc

Once you are comfortable with this easy form, you may not want to use the armrests for support that much—only when needed.

The next variation of this exercise lets you do the squats with your arms crossed over your chest. Again, complete three sets of ten squats with a one-minute break between sets.

Now you can progress to the next option: squats with weights. Here you will want to use five-pound dumbbells in each hand and proceed as before. Start with this relatively low weight first, and progress slowly.

Here is a link to a video for squats with dumbbells:

https://www.youtube.com/watch?v=RLM0uWaRaGU

When you start with your strength training, do not exceed five minutes of push-ups and squats in the first little while. Allow time, and then increase to ten minutes.

It cannot be emphasized enough to take it easy with the weights, whether you work out at home or at the gym. Build your program over time. This not only prevents frustration, but—much more importantly—it also prevents injury. Also remember, beyond a time of forty-five minutes, your body will feel the excessive stress and sound the alarm bell, meaning that the release of the stress hormones (ACTH and cortisol) will be triggered (Sears 2000, p.100). Instead of creating fitness for your body and benefit for your health, you have axed the benefit and produced a disbalance in your hormonal status. This is a direct highway to accelerate the aging process. So take pauses of fifteen minutes or longer if you really want to exercise intensely. It would be better in this situation to exercise up to forty-five minutes in the morning and do the same again in the evening.

The following table provides a good very basic plan to achieve a level of fitness on an ongoing basis. You can achieve it by consistent daily exercise.

Basic exercise plan

1. Aerobic exercise for 30 minutes

2. Upper- and lower-body strength training for 5 to 10 minutes each

If you want to create a more intense program, you can do the following:

- aerobic exercise (bicycle, treadmill, brisk power walk) that burns 300 calories

- weight training at home or at the gym 3 times per week, but not exceeding 45 minutes

- flexibility training: stretches, yoga, Pilates

Stretching before exercise is an excellent warm-up. It can also prevent muscle cramps. Stretching after a vigorous walk is also very relaxing. You can build stretching easily into your daily routine. After sitting for an extended period, you will very likely have the urge to stretch and loosen up those muscles. We do not have to look far for examples. Although as humans we seem to have unlearned how to stretch, cats are natural talents!

The following is a link to a good summary video about various stretches; choose the ones you are comfortable with:

https://www.youtube.com/watch?v=-iY5V0xiiKw

Building fitness into our daily routines

Most important is our awareness of fitness and making the choice to build it into our daily routines. You can make the choice at home and at work as indicated in the following table:

Ten practical ways to incorporate fitness into your routine

1. Use the stairs at work instead of taking the elevator.
2. Walk to the corner store if you can. Go for a walk during your lunch break
3. Walk with your dog.
4. Take up a hobby like dancing, aerobic dancing, square dancing, or line dancing.
5. Buy or rent a fitness video, and enjoy a workout at home. It beats the winter doldrums.
6. Do some tai chi.
7. Join a local sports club (e.g., tennis, softball, pickleball).
8. Whether you go for a walk alone or with a few neighbors does not matter, but go for a brisk walk!
9. Put the remote control away when you watch TV. Get out of that chair instead to walk to the TV and back.
10. Rake the grass clippings and the leaves instead of buying a leaf blower. Similarly, sweep your driveway!

Summary regarding physical fitness

We are not born as couch potatoes. If you watch children, you will notice that they love to jump, run, climb, and dance. They obviously enjoy being alive and active, and so should you. You are never too old to have fun, and it is never too late, either. If you've seen people exercising with exhaustion and agony in their faces and have come to the conclusion that true exercise means heroics and suffering, you are missing the boat. The aspect of stress and cortisol release has been explained already. Too much of a good thing is not a good thing anymore. Overdoses do not work; I don't care what overdose we are talking about. And anything that is exaggeration and translates into "pure torture" will not stand up in time. The result can be the extreme of injury. At the very least, exercise will become a tedious duty, and you'll be sick and tired of everlasting muscle aches and quit. Exercise frenzies remain a fad that lose their charm pretty fast. Make exercise fun by introducing various activities, gradually building strength and endurance, and enjoying a variety of exercise options, and you will be successful reaping the benefits over a lifetime. Whether you enjoy solitary walks or you have more fun joining a group is strictly up to you, and you will find what works best for you. The next time you watch a cat stretching luxuriously or some children jumping and dancing, see it as a special invitation to yourself to be alive and active and have fun while you do it!

Chapter 6:
The Stress Factor

Fitness for the mind (stress management and relaxation techniques)
Physical fitness is important, as the previous chapter has explained, but the mind and body are an interrelated, connected unit. Physical well-being translates into positive emotions: it greatly contributes to feeling well and enjoying activities, adding zest and vibrancy to our lives, no matter how old or how young we are. While some people are unable to enjoy an activity like running, walking, or dancing due to a physical handicap, very often persons with enormous physical challenges can inspire us with their positive attitudes.

Our mind-set has a profound influence on our body. We all have experienced events that disrupt our comfortable routine, such as taking an examination. In response to such situations, we experience physical symptoms: our palms feel clammy, our heart beats like a hammer, and we may notice a slight tremor of our hands. The feelings start with our frame of mind, and they translate into stress. Our brains send signals, and in response the body releases the stress hormone. In the remote past, when our ancestors existed as hunters and gatherers, this

77

hormonal response got them ready to face dangerous, wild animals and run for their lives. Giving their last reserves enabled our ancestors to bring home food for the tribe. We are not facing these kinds of difficulties, yet our bodies react the same way in situations that we perceive as menacing. We call it stress. We are no longer fighting wild animals, but dealing with time pressures, meeting deadlines, sitting in rush-hour traffic, moving a household, negotiating a salary increase, or having a disagreement with a family member can cause the same hormonal responses. What is worse, a hormonal reponse, which should only occur in extraordinary situations, becomes a common occurrence. We call that being stressed out, and it does not feel good.

What does this response do to our bodies? Cortisol, the stress hormone, is a powerful aging substance. When we collapse in an armchair after an especially harrowing day and declare that we feel as if we are a hundred years old, this statement is not so farfetched. Continuous stress ages us prematurely. Our immune system gets weakened. It is not uncommon to get sick at the holidays or during the first few days of a trip. In both instances we are likely stressed to the limit, and we are coming down with the flu. Stress comes in many disguises. It can challenge us with events like the loss of a loved one, a meeting with a disagreeable supervisor, or an encounter with a rude driver that cuts us off and shows us the finger. But stress can also occur with a winning lottery ticket, a long-awaited dream vacation, or the birth of a new baby.

To put it quite simply, there is good stress and bad stress. It is present in all life situations, and since it pervades our daily lives, it would be ridiculous to assume that we can avoid it. What we can do is live with stress. The term *stress management* has become a buzzword. It refers to learning to manage stressful situations rather than allowing stress to run our lives. When we study the lives of our ancestors, we notice that they lived through wars, natural disasters, financial hardships, and personal losses. Yet a lot of these people managed to survive these adversities and still retain their zest for life and their positive outlook. Of course, there were others who turned angry, bitter, resentful, and negative. The difference can be found in how each of them managed—or mismanaged—stress.

Sleep

Sleep is the natural counterbalance to stress. During the hours of sleep, the brain has time to unwind, and the body can reset the control mechanism for our hormone glands in the hypothalamus. Growth hormone, the stress hormones (CRH, ACTH, and cortisol), and more are recharged overnight while we sleep. But if we interfere with the circadian rhythm by working night shifts, traveling through more than one or two time zones, or celebrating too long into the night, we pay a price the following day, if not one or two weeks. Sleep hygiene is important for staying grounded. Dr. Perlmutter describes a study that showed a reduction in leptin levels by 20 percent caused by sleep deprivation, which in turn caused a 24 percent increase in appetite for refined carbohydrates (sweets), salty snacks, and starchy foods (Perlmutter, 2013). In obese people leptin and insulin are both increased, and insulin and leptin resistance develop, making hormone balance that much more difficult. Add to this another hormone from the stomach, ghrelin, which is secreted when your stomach is hungry. Sleep deprivation leads to higher levels of ghrelin, making you more hungry, but leptin resistance will make you not feel satisfied with normal portion sizes, so the appetite center in your brain will demand more food even when objectively you have had enough. There are no drugs to rebalance this. But there is a simple nondrug method: get enough sleep, change from refined carbohydrates (sugars and starchy foods) to complex carbohydrates (vegetables and fruit), and exercise.

Coping with stress is not a one-shot deal, yet this approach is not uncommon: you may have experienced a situation during which you were stretched to the limit. Yet you put up with it day after day because you consoled yourself with the plan of a holiday at the end. There is certainly nothing wrong with a holiday, but when you reached this goal, you probably were feeling totally exhausted. You do yourself more of a favor by setting some time aside every day to unwind from stressful situations and relax. Various publications about stress management exist, and many of them are excellent resources for self-help.

The other part you can do is learn relaxation exercises. Several techniques you can use are listed below.

Breathing exercises (and yoga)

Relaxation occurs when we concentrate on our body positions and breathing patterns. This has been practiced for centuries and is known as yoga. Yoga courses are offered in many communities, and it can be practiced at home as well.

To practice yoga wear comfortable clothing. Find a comfortable position sitting in a comfortable recliner chair, or lie on your back. Put one hand on your stomach and the other on your chest. Close your eyes and inhale slowly and deeply through your nose. As you do, notice which hand is rising and falling with each breath. Exhale through your mouth. Do not hunch your shoulders or move your chest: the breathing is done with your abdomen. Focus on the sensation of the warm, relaxing air flowing into your body, and imagine that the warmth spreads all over your body. Continue to focus on this feeling of relaxation as every muscle in your body becomes more and more relaxed.

Meditation

With meditation you allow your conscious thinking to take a rest. It is like switching off your left hemisphere that does your thinking and allowing your right hemisphere, the brain that knows about art and music to take over for awhile.

To encourage this, sit in a comfortable position on a chair, or choose a cross-legged position on the floor. You can lie down if sitting is not comfortable for you. Focus on stillness: sit (or lie) as still as possible. Breathe in slowly and deeply. Exhale slowly, and focus on a sound as you exhale. You may want to choose a meaningful word or a short phrase. You will probably relate best to a word that has spiritual significance to you. As you hum this "mantra," allow your feelings and sensations to drift in and out of your mind. If you find that your thoughts wander to something other than your breathing, refocus yourself. Don't get anxious: it takes practice. You will notice that this quiet exercise will make you feel very peaceful, and you will give your mind a chance to quiet down.

Meditation in religion

Meditation is practiced in many religions. The Jesus Prayer ("Lord Jesus Christ, Son of God, have mercy on me, the sinner") has been used for centuries in the Christian faith, and the chanting of a single syllable like *om* has been part of spiritual exercises in the East. Daily prayer is a boundless source of peace and inner healing. You can use an original prayer, thanking for life's blessings, forgiving others, forgiving yourself, and letting go of pain and guilt. Or choose a meaningful prayer from a devotional book that is dear to you. You will discover what inspires and lifts you up. Make it part of your life.

We do not need a lot of time to practice meditation. Often meditation is associated with thoughts of sitting on a mat and chanting for hours on end or going to a retreat for several days. There is nothing wrong with a retreat or unhurried, restorative time away from the daily grind. But the most important thing is to allow time on a daily basis. Pick twenty to thirty minutes that belong to you. You may have a break during the day or take time to wind down at the end of a busy day. Some even prefer the serene quietness of the early morning. It does not matter when, but do it, and give your mind the quiet time it needs on a daily basis.

Self-Hypnosis

Self-hypnosis is another relaxation technique. First, some myths about hypnosis need to be addressed and clarified.

Some of us may have seen a show that featured stage hypnosis: a group of volunteers went on stage and, at the suggestion of the stage hypnotist, started to act like musicians or dancers or just looked like they were totally out of it. Immediately we shake our heads at the very idea of hypnosis. Brainwashing, losing control, and not knowing what we are doing come to mind, and this does not sound like a good idea to us.

Clinical hypnosis is not designed to get us out of control at all. We are in control; we are merely allowing our mind to slip into another ego state. Normally we rely on the left side of our brain in our intellectual functioning, provided that we are right-hand dominant. (If we are left-hand dominant, the right hemisphere is the one mostly utilized). When we allow ourselves to become deeply relaxed, the other side of the brain becomes active: if you are right-handed, the right side of the brain is more active in a deep state of relaxation. A technician who is trained to read EEG tests (which can measure brain-wave activity) will recognize a different wave pattern the moment you enter into a relaxed state. This is the technicality.

Now let's look at the practical side of being in an altered state. There is nothing complicated about it. It's easy.In fact, you have switched to this state many times in your life. I'll give you one example. You leave the house, and a mile away you wonder whether you switched the lights off (or the iron or another appliance). You turn around and go back home to prevent trouble, but when you check, all is well: the lights are off, and the appliance is switched off. You did it automatically. A similar event could be an animated conversation on the telephone or time spent with some friends. Before you know it, an hour or more has elapsed. You wonder where the time went. It passed, but you did not notice it, as you were entirely focused on the conversation.

What follows would be a suitable exercise for intentional self-hypnosis. You will soon find out that it can be like a power nap. It is a skill you can use to unwind from a day and fall into a comfortable sleep. You may even want to use it to relax after a stressful morning at work. Relaxation cassettes or discs can be very beneficial and are easy to use, as the voice of the therapist can help you achieve a state of deep relaxation. You should, however, never attempt to listen to a cassette or disc when you are driving or operating machinery!

*You can practice self-hypnosis alone or with the help of a self-hyp-
nosis cassette or disc, Here is a sample text:*

Sit in a comfortable recliner chair, or lie down in a comfortable spot.
Close your eyes, and breathe in and out slowly and deeply. Visualize
yourself at the most relaxing place you can envisage. You may envisage yourself lying on a warm, sandy beach or at some other serene
setting. Now imagine the clear, blue sky with white clouds high above.
Put yourself onto one of those clouds, and drift, slowly and gently,
into a state of profound and satisfying relaxation. You can count
from ten backward to one: Ten…you are letting the muscles in your
neck become soft and letting all the tension go. Nine…let the warm,
relaxed feeling flow into your arms and all the way to your finger-
tips. Eight…as you continue to breathe in and out deeply, the feeling
of relaxation flows into your chest and into your abdomen. All the
time you drift more and more, deeper and deeper, relaxing. Seven…
allowing yourself to rest, nothing concerns you, nothing interrupts
you, and you enjoy the quiet and peaceful feeling of letting go. Six…
the sense of rest and relaxation fills you with gentle warmth, which
expands to the muscles of your thighs and your legs, all the way to
your toes. Five…as your muscles are relaxed from head to toe and
your mind is free from all daily concerns, you let the warm wave of
relaxation carry you. Four…relaxing more and more. Three…drifting,
floating, and relaxing. Two…you are taking all the quiet, the sense of
peace, and the calmness that fills your mind as you prepare for your
work and for returning from your journey into this relaxed state. You
become aware of the sounds around you as you feel yourself waking
up. One…fully awake now, rested and comfortable.

If you are concerned about how much time you need to invest
in such an exercise, you can be assured that you will not need hours
and hours. Twenty to thirty minutes will be ample. Find the relaxation

technique that appeals to you most, or meditate and incorporate breathing exercises. These are some examples of useful activities for meditation or relaxation. As with any exercise, you will get better with practice and will find more benefits to your emotional well-being as you go on.

Anger and hostility are not only emotions that make your life and that of others miserable. Anger and hostility are risk factors for heart disease. Hostile individuals are on a potential suicide mission. They are five times more at a risk to die before the age of fifty than people who are not hostile and do not get mad at the drop of a hat! Anger and hostility are risk factors for heart disease. Dr. Amen, a well-known psychiatrist who uses special brain scans for assessments, called single-photon emission computerized tomography (SPECT) to investigate brain function has accumulated over 80,000 SPECT scans of brains of patients. I was at a lecture where Dr. Amen was the keynote speaker and remarked that SPECT scans can show a distinct image in an angry, hostile individual. People with this condition have a disbalanced brain pattern. Here is an example from Dr. Amens's website of a fourteen-year-old male who had an anger problem, but could be successfully calmed down with appropriate medication:

http://www.amenclinics.com/the-science/spect-gallery/item/angersevere-odd#page

You can learn to avoid escalations into rage attacks and shouting matches; you can rethink a statement instead of blowing up. You can also learn to laugh at a situation. If anger becomes an obstacle that is too big to handle, you may benefit from cognitive therapy and counseling. Remember, you do not have to embark alone on a difficult journey!

Dr. Amen also talked about taking care of the "ants", those annoying little negative thoughts that creep in during the course of a day. Stop yourelf when you think negatively. Start concentrating more on the positive, and don't make it a habit to expect disaster. For example, you may want to stop watching the eleven o'clock news before you go to sleep. Often you are not hearing or seeing wonderful things that contribute to a restful sleep!

Put humor into your life. Laughter helps to release frustration, and it releases endorphins, the feel-good hormones. Humor also helps us cope with the unavoidable stressors we encounter in day-to-day living.

And finally, be affectionate and empathic (without conditions attached) toward people around you, and love and accept yourself.

Achieving and maintaining fitness of the mind is an ongoing project, a lifelong task. It comes down to learning some exercises that promote emotional well-being and help us cope with stress. We can learn meditation and relaxation. But we must also get to know ourselves more intimately and examine our habits, thought patterns, and attitudes. For anybody, there will be surprises, wonderful discoveries, and inspiring benefits. The small daily steps ultimately make this a fascinating journey with profound insights into our mental and physical functions and how they work together in harmony.

Chapter 7:
Hormones Are Everything:
Bioidentical Hormone Replacement

Hormones have a profound effect on our body composition. Muscles are built up by testosterone, which is the main hormone in men but is also important in smaller amounts in women. Women's main sex hormones are estrogen and progesterone, which will be discussed further below. Apart from these hormones, thyroid hormones need to be balanced, as a lack of them leads to hypothyroidism with weight gain. Besides these hormones, there is the leptin/ghrelin system, which regulates body mass by the interplay of ghrelin and leptin. When ghrelin is low, we get hungry and want to eat, and when leptin is produced by fat cells, we are satisfied and stop eating. As mentioned in chapter 6, sleep deprivation can lead to an overproduction of ghrelin (produced by the stomach, making you feel hungry) and leptin (produced by fat cells, making you feel hungry as well). Added to this, chronic overfeeding with refined carbs (sugar, starches, bread, grains, and so on) leads to leptin and insulin resistance, which interferes with the off switch of your appetite center (Perlmutter, 2013). Getting enough sleep, switching to unrefined carbohydrates, and avoiding low-fat diets will rebalance the ghrelin/leptin system.

Without getting further into detail, it is important to note that hormones need to be in balance. As we age above forty-five to fifty, both men and women experience various hormone deficiencies as part of the aging process. However, research in Europe over the past fifty years and research in the United States over the past twenty-five years has shown that replacement with bioidentical hormones can normalize our hormone balance.

Bioidentical hormone replacement prolongs life. What follows is a more detailed look at what such hormone replacement looks like for both women and men. Before I continue, I want to stress that I am talking about replacing what is missing and replacing only with natural hormones, not some artificial hormone derivative produced by a drug company. The reason this is immensely important is that hormone receptors in the body are distributed all over our vital organs, including bones, blood vessels, and the nervous system. If there is no lock-and-key fit (meaning the bioidentical hormone fits the hormone receptor), there is trouble: the Women's Health Initiative in 2002 used synthetic hormones for hormone replacement therapy that did not fit the hormone receptors, and this caused many problems, including heart attacks, strokes, osteoporosis, cancer (NIH site on Women's Health Initiative).

Physiology of aging

As we age, we gradually produce fewer hormones in our hormone glands, but the various hormone glands deteriorate in their functions at different rates. Beyond the age of thirty, we produce less melatonin and less growth hormone. As a result our sleep pattern may change, as melatonin is necessary for a deep sleep. The decreasing growth hormone production means that we lose some of our muscle mass and accumulate more fat in the subcutaneous tissues. At thirty-five to forty, our adrenal glands produce less DHEA, a hormone that is a precursor to our sex hormones in males and females. The gonads (testicles and ovaries) also produce fewer hormones, a process that starts five years before menopause and about five years before andropause (the male menopause equivalent).

Typically a woman will enter menopause between the ages of forty-five and fifty-five, at which time her periods stop and postmenopausal symptoms begin to interfere with her well-being. Men enter andropause (the male equivalent of menopause) at the age of fifty-five to sixty-five, at which time erectile dysfunction occurs and often the individual will become the stereotype grumpy old man. Other hormones, such as thyroid hormones, are also affected by the slowdown. Hypothyroidism is common in people above the age of fifty.

Baseline laboratory tests

In order to know what is going on, the physician or naturopath needs to order a number of tests to assess whether there is inflammation and how your key hormone levels are. The cardiovascular system markers should also be checked, the liver enzymes and vitamin D_3 level. Inflammatory markers are fasting insulin levels and C-reactive protein (CRP). Fasting cholesterol and subfractions (HDL, LDL, VDLP, small LDL) and fasting triglycerides are also measured. Thyroid hormones (T3 and T4, TSH) are measured to rule out overfunction or under function. Typically hypothyroidism is found, which would have to be rectified by taking Armour (a mix of T3 and T4 thyroid hormones).

At this point I need to explain that a long time ago, research by Dr. Lee showed that progesterone hormone levels are notoriously unreliable when blood tests are done. Levels of the other sex hormones and cortisol are also not that reliable with blood tests. For this reason, saliva hormone tests have been invented that conveniently report a panel of five hormones from one saliva sample: DHEAS (which is the storage form of DHEA), estradiol (the major estrogen in a woman), progesterone, testosterone, and cortisol. The saliva hormone tests correlate very well with the actual tissue hormone levels. You can order saliva tests through Dr. Lee's website (Dr. John Lee's website). Another long-standing lab in the United States is Dr. David Zava's lab (ZRT Laboratory). In Canada the Rocky Mountain Analytical Lab can process your saliva tests (Rocky Mountain Analytical website).

Women's hormone replacement

Let us say that a woman is experiencing postmenopausal symptoms and considering bioidentical hormone replacement. The physician will want to first rule out insulin resistance by ordering a fasting insulin level. If this is normal and the other baseline tests are normal as well (except for missing estrogen and progesterone) the physician will usually start to replace progesterone first, using a bioidentical hormone cream to be applied once or twice per day. If estrogen levels are also low, the next step in four weeks or so is to add Bi-Est, a bioidentical estrogen replacement cream. After eight weeks of hormone replacement, the saliva hormone test is repeated to see whether the estrogen and progesterone levels have come up and whether the ratio of progesterone to estrogen is at least 200 or more. Dr. Lee has extensively researched this and found that women with a ratio of less than 200 to 1 (progesterone/estrogen ratio) were more prone to breast cancer. He also stated that there are three basic rules with regard to bioidentical hormone replacement (Dr. Lee website, bioidentical hormones): (1) only replace hormones when they are measured to be low, (2) use only bioidentical hormones (never synthetic), and (3) only replace with low doses of bioidentical hormones to bring hormone levels to physiological levels (body levels that were experienced to be normal before).

Many women whose hormones are not replaced during menopause have estrogen dominance, meaning that their progesterone/estrogen ratio is less than 200:1, which puts these women at risk of developing breast cancer. Women who are overweight or obese also are estrogen dominant (from estrogen produced in excess through aromatase in the fatty tissue, explained further below), which makes them more prone to breast cancer, uterine cancer, and colon cancer. Without bioidentical hormone replacement, inflammatory processes take place in the joints (causing arthritis), in the nervous system (causing Alzheimer's and dementia), and in the blood vessels (causing heart attacks and strokes). Rebalancing your hormones to a youthful state by paying attention to the hormone levels and the hormone ratios mentioned will remove the inflammatory reactions and reduce the risk for cancer.

Men's hormone replacement

Males enter andropause ten to fifteen years later than women enter menopause. Typically testosterone production slows down, leading to hair loss, erectile dysfunction, loss of muscle mass, osteoporosis, and Alzheimer's/dementia. Blood tests (bioavailable testosterone) or saliva tests are both reliable in determining a deficiency. Replacement with bioidentical hormone creams once per day is the preferred method of treatment. Overweight and obese men produce significant amounts of estrogen through an enzyme localized in fatty tissue, called aromatase (William Faloon, 2008). Aromatase converts testosterone and other male hormones, called androgens, into estrogen. Estrogen causes breast growth, weakens muscles, and leads to abdominal fat accumulation, heart disease, and strokes.

While the progesterone/estrogen ratio is important in women, there is a different ratio for men, the testosterone/estrogen ratio. This should be in the twenty to forty range for a man to feel good and energetic. Unfortunately, many men over the age of fifty-five have testosterone/estrogen ratios much lower than twenty. This makes them more prone to heart disease and prostate cancer (Lee, 2007). Finally, a male also does need a small amount of estrogen and normal thyroid hormones as well as all of the other hormones for the "hormonal symphony" (Somers, 2008) that will allow him to function at his best.

Safety of hormone replacement

Otherwise reputable websites still state that bioidentical hormones are not safer than standard synthetic hormones. This confuses the consumer and does not serve the public well. I much prefer the text of the *Wikipedia*, which offers a more thorough review regarding the safety of hormone replacement and explains what the issues are (Wikipedia re. bioidentical hormone replacement and NIH site on Women's Health Initiative).

In the United States, there is a collective experience of about twenty-five years on thousands of patients, but there have not been any randomized studies, as Big Pharma, who would have the money to finance such studies, is not interested in proving that bioidentical drugs would be safer than their distorted synthetic hormone copies that do not fit the body's hormone receptors. There are some noble exceptions: Big Pharma is now producing bioidentical insulin and human growth hormone, both of which were determined to be safe in toxicity studies. In Europe, bioidentical hormones have been used since the sixties and on a larger scale since the seventies. So the European experience of safe use of bioidentical hormones is presently about forty to fifty years (Virginia Hopkins : open letter to Oprah).

The FDA is contributing to the confusion of the public, as can be seen from this publication (Conaway, 2011). One example of this is the progesterone product Prometrium, a bioidentical micronized progesterone capsule that can be taken by mouth. By law the manufacturer had to put a warning label on the package identical to that on progestin, the synthetic, nonbioidentical hormone that has been shown to have severe side effects. As explained in the paper by Conaway Prometrium should not have been required to have a warning label, for bioidentical hormones are the safest form of hormone replacement and if administered in the right ratios, will actually prevent cancer and premature cardiovascular and joint deterioration. In other words, bioidentical hormone replacement can add many years of useful life when started before permanent organ damage sets in from the aging process (which would be due to missing hormones). Here is another review of the safety record of bioidentical hormone replacement: (Female hormone restoration: link under references).

Why bother with hormone replacement?

Nature has a plan of knocking us off to make room for the next generation. The only way that you can change nature's plan to kill us prematurely through cardiovascular disease, arthritis, dementia, and loss of sex life is by bioidentical hormone replacement. Of course you also need the other ingredients known to prolong life, such as healthy (preferably organic) foods, exercise, and detoxification. Many women are scared to treat the hormone deficiencies that cause their menopausal symptoms because of the Women's Health Initiative's results with synthetic hormones. Men who would benefit from testosterone are often anxious that they may get prostate cancer, when in reality it is the exact opposite as Dr. Morgentaler from Harvard University has shown in several publications: testosterone prevents prostate cancer (Morgentaler, 2008). Also, women who may take much smaller amounts of testosterone have never been shown to develop any cancer from that (your body is used to this hormone).

Conclusion

In this chapter I have summarized information about bioidentical hormone replacement in some detail in order to clarify this often-misunderstood topic. Don't get confused by the FDA or highbrow medical websites. Big Pharma has a powerful lobby that attempts to keep the medical profession in the belief that its products are better than those that nature has provided (I call it "defend your patent rights"). We are still in a flux state in which anybody who tells the truth about hormones is met with much criticism. In another few decades, the benefits of bioidentical hormones will be an accepted fact, and people will wonder why the Women's Health Initiative was done without a control with bioidentical hormones. With bioidentical hormone replacement, you can add about twenty years of youthful life without disabilities to the normal life expectancy. Exercise, detoxification, and consumption of organic food with avoidance of wheat, starch, and sugar can add another five to ten years. The baby boomers are lucky that they have this new tool to prolong life. I wonder whether they will put it to good use.

Chapter 8:
Vitamins and Supplements

Vitamins have long been recognized as an essential part of the nutrition team. From the tentative groping when sailors recognized that limes prevented scurvy to the solid research data surrounding vitamin C by Linus Pauling, we have come a long way.

There is a catalogue of vitamin preparations, minerals, and supplements available to us, and vitamin sales are no longer the domain of health-food stores: supermarkets have a section of vitamins and nutritional supplements, and the variety can be confusing to the consumer. Yet it is a fallacy to believe that we must acquire all the varieties in capsule or tablet form. With proper food intake, we can get the essential vitamins and minerals. In doing so we go back to Hippocrates, who suggested that food be our medicine.

With today's knowledge base, we have a fairly clear understanding of how vitamin supplementation prolongs life. Life expectancy seems to be determined genetically and depends on the telomere length. The telomere, a small appendix to the chromosomes in each cell, assists in cell division and stability. At birth our telomeres are at their longest; with each cell division, the telomeres shorten a tiny bit.

Xu and co-workers have provided the first evidence based on a large population that daily vitamin supplements led to 5.1 percent longer telomeres (Xu, 2009). This translates into 9.8 years of longer life expectancy for those taking vitamins compared to those who do not supplement. The same study also found that micronutrients from food were not related to telomere length with the exception of vitamin C and E. The authors concluded that multivitamin use is associated with slower biological aging due to longer telomeres.

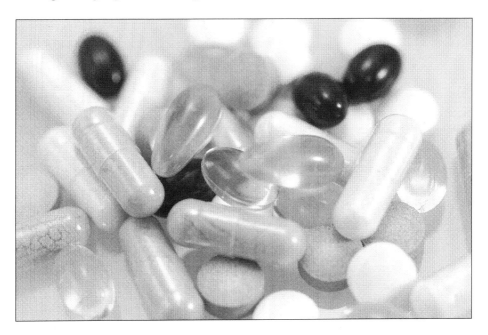

It was known since 1961 hat in our lifetime each cell could only perform so many cell divisions (the Hayflick limit, see Wiki citation under references). Another life-limiting factor is the state of our mitochondria, particles within each living cell that provide energy and participate in cell communication and in our body's metabolism (About.com biology regarding mitochondria). We are born with a set of mitochondria inherited directly from our mother and grandmother, an instance of non-Mendelian genetic transmission. Although our fathers contribute 50 percent to the cell nucleus DNA (Mendelian inheritance), this is not the case with regard to the DNA of the mitochondria, of which 100 percent is derived from the ovum of our mothers. The reason for this is that only the head of the sperm enters the ovum upon fertilization of the egg. The sperm's tail, which does contain a few mitochondria for energy, does not. This is the reason longevity is transmitted by ways of the maternal genetic line from generation to generation. Unfortunately the DNA of the mitochondria comes only as one maternal set, making it more vulnerable to damage by free radicals. The DNA of the cell nucleus comes in double strands (one from your father, one from your mother), and some repair kits are included that come in handy when there is minor damage to the DNA by free radicals: these tools that the body uses for DNA repair are glutathione from the liver and vitamin C from food and supplements that provide powerful antioxidant activity that supports cells and mitochondria. The cells in the body that contain the most mitochondria per cell are the tissues of the brain, heart, muscles, liver, and kidneys. This may be the reason with aging (meaning loss of mitochondria in tissues) people often die from Alzheimer's disease, heart attacks, liver failure, kidney failure, and falls related to muscle weakness.

Under the best of circumstances (good genetics, healthy lifestyle, good nutrition, regular moderate exercise, and natural hormone supplementation to prevent premature aging) we are still limited to a life expectancy of not more than about 120 years. If you incorporate the supplements listed below, your chances are much better to reach this goal due to the positive effects on your telomeres and mitochondria.

Preventing chronic inflammation

As stated before, chronic inflammation can cause cardiovascular disease, diabetes, arthritis, cancer, lung disease (asthma and COPD), neurological disease (Parkinson's disease, Alzheimer's disease, and possibly MS), and autoimmune diseases. The antioxidant vitamins and detoxification described below will aid in preventing chronic inflammation. However, it is also important to eliminate or limit sugar intake and starchy food intake (noodles, rice, potatoes, bread, and cakes) to prevent insulin hypersecretion, which causes the metabolic syndrome and leads to chronic inflammation. A physician can order a fasting insulin level to check for hyperinsulinism.

Detoxification

Before you supplement, the body needs to be detoxified so that the nutrients and supplements can access the cells and do their supportive work. Books like *Breakthrough* by Suzanne Somers have reviewed newer insights of antiaging medicine, including the importance of ridding the body of heavy metals like mercury, lead, and cadmium. Chelation therapy with vitamin C and glutathione or with EDTA can be used to remove some of these heavy toxic metals.

In a May 2013 blog entitled "Get rid of toxins safely" I have reviewed several detoxification methods in more detail (http://www.askdrray.com/get-rid-of-toxins-safely/)

Briefly, there is fasting, colonics including coffee enemas, skin detoxification including saunas and Epsom salt baths, herbal use for supposed kidney detoxification and the ultimate detoxification with intravenous chelating substances.

About using vitamins and supplements

Undeniably there are times when vitamins should be supplemented. For instance, patients with pernicious anemia benefit from vitamin B_{12} injections. In addition, pregnant mothers are encouraged to take prenatal vitamin supplements. A crucial supplement in pregnancy is folic acid, which reduces the likelihood of spina bifida in the baby. It is further known that in infancy the baby will not get enough vitamin D_3 in milk, and accordingly the vitamin is administered as drops in a bit of formula or baby food. Vitamin C has also been associated with benefits in the cold and flu season. Multivitamin preparations are of importance when our food intake is just not quite enough to meet the demands: pregnancy, as discussed before, is such a situation, but breastfeeding a baby puts high demands on the nursing mother as well.

Anybody recovering from an illness will likewise benefit from a multivitamin supplement, and anyone who is not eating properly, which can be the case during stress or travel, will do well using a well-balanced vitamin supplement. Vitamins are not miracle drugs, but they can boost our resistance to illness and contribute to our well-being. Consider them insurance. They can be your ally, but you still have to do your part with good nutrition and a healthy lifestyle. Do not fall into the trap of starting your day with a big array of supplements. More is usually not better, and exaggerated doses of vitamins can be harmful: for instance, huge doses of vitamin A will have toxic effects on your liver, which is not exactly a prescription for health and energy. Too much calcium can significantly raise your risk for developing kidney stones. This does not mean that you should turn around and avoid any vitamin supplement. What you need is balance and moderation, whether you're considering food intake or supplements. This has been only a brief overview regarding vitamins and supplements, and this information is summarized in the table below as well. However, many reliable websites discuss this topic in much more detail (CNN Interactive: vitamin guide).

One of the more interesting new developments is supplementation with amino acids, which are supposed to help the body build up the human growth hormone (HGH), which may postpone aging. Some literature refutes this use, saying that exercise can trigger the production of your own HGH in the presence of normal protein intake. Protein is broken down into amino acids in the gut during the digestive process, and the body absorbs the amino acids and produces HGH in the pituitary gland. Exercise has long been recognized as a factor in HGH production and longevity.

As stated before, most of your vitamins will come from your food. There are some vitamins that act as a form of insurance, contributing to your health (Sears 2000, p. 276):

VITAMINS AND SUPPLEMENTS, YOUR BASIC LIFE INSURANCE

VITAMIN/SUPPLEMENT	USES
Fish Oil	• important for omega-3 fatty acids • can be taken in capsule form or as oil • 400 mg of EPA (eicosapentaenoic acid) and about 200 mg of DHA (docosahexaenoic acid) per capsule • 2–3 per day • should be mainly omega-3 (often omega-6 mixed in) • should be molecularly distilled to remove cancer-producing herbicides, pesticides, and heavy metals
Vitamin E	• associated with a healthy heart • there are several different tocopherols, which go under the name of vitamin E. Most vitamin E capsules from the health food store will contain a mix of alpha, gamma, beta and delta tocopherols. It is a powerful anti-inflammatory. • 400 IU of the mix per day
Vitamin C	• the "antioxidant" vitamin • associated with protection against colds and flus in winter • promotes wound healing • Ester C better absorbed • 1,000 mg daily
Calcium and Magnesium	• important for everybody • associated with bone health and important for post-menopausal females 250 mg of each twice a day • vitamin K2 (see below) also beneficial

Vitamin B complex	<ul><li>the "stress" vitamin</li><li>amply found in vegetables</li><li>take one B-100 capsule per day when diet does not contain enough greens and vegetables</li></ul>
Multivitamin supplements	<ul><li>often recommended when nutrition is not adequate (or with pregnancy, breast feeding, or recovery from illness)</li><li>Vitamin A (about 3,500 IU)</li><li>Vitamins B1, B2, B3, B5, B6, and B12, as well as folic acid and Biotin would be useful to take as a multivitamin supplement</li><li>take as tablets or in liquid form on a daily basis.</li></ul>
Resveratrol	<ul><li>antioxidants that occur in the skins of grapes, often combined with ellagic acid (e.g. in Trophic)</li><li>a powerful antioxidant</li><li>prevents heart disease and cancers; 200 mg to 250 mg per day</li></ul>
Coenzyme Q10	<ul><li>200 mg per day up to the age of 50</li><li>400 mg per day when over 50</li><li>Supports heart health and is vital for cellular energy production (supports mitochondria)</li></ul>
Vitamin D3	<ul><li>this has been recently found to be very powerful in preventing a multitude of cancers</li><li>2,000 IU or more (best 4,000 to 5,000 IU) once per day</li></ul>
D-Ribose	<ul><li>this is a special sugar that supports cell metabolism</li><li>a flat teaspoon once per day increases energy and endurance</li><li>in fibromyalgia it may give some relief for pain in higher doses (a flat teaspoon two to three times per day)</li></ul>

Melatonin	<ul><li>important for the body to recuperate, very valuable to enhance restful sleep and a powerful antioxidant. It actually is a hormone from the pineal gland, and it makes other hormones work better (thyroid and steroid hormones, important in antiaging medicine)</li><li>take 1 to 3 mg at bedtime</li><li>safe to take up to 10 mg per day. You may experience nightmares for up to 1 week initially when starting on it (harmless)</li></ul>
L- Carnosine	<ul><li>good support to cell function and assisting neurological function</li><li>1 or 2 capsules (500 mg capsules) per day</li></ul>
L-Carnitine	<ul><li>not an antioxidant, but a good support for muscles, including the heart</li><li>two 500 mg capsules per day used for antiaging</li></ul>
Alpha Lipoic Acid	<ul><li>100 mg per day are a desirable addition to the regimen you are already taking</li></ul>
Phosphatidyl Serine	<ul><li>Probably one of the best weapons against cognitive decline</li><li>100 mg per day for prevention purposes in persons without cognitive decline</li><li>200 to 300 mg for early Alzheimer's patients</li><li>with the higher doses a bitter taste sensation can occur (harmless); simply reduce the dose</li></ul>
Vitamin K2	<ul><li>prevents hardening of the arteries and osteoporosis</li><li>100 to 200 micrograms per day</li><li>This blog explains in detail how it works: http://www.askdrray.com/calcium-vitamin-d3-and-vitamin-k2-needed-for-bone-health/</li></ul>

Io-Plex SR	• iodine prevents cell damage from chlorinated water, bromide contamination of our environment (like hot tubs), from pasta and bread (products made from flour that has bromide in it). If you eat bread, burgers, pasta, and the like, consider iodine supplements (Brownstein, 2009) • This iodine preparation from Kripp's Pharmacy, Vancouver, BC, contains 5 mg of elemental iodine and 7.5 mg of iodide per capsule. • 12.5 mg capsule twice per day
Vitamin B-2 (riboflavin)	• together with niacinamide and iodide, it stabilizes the cell metabolism • One tablet (100 mg) per day
Vitamin B-3 (niacinamide)	• together with vitamin B2, it stimulates oxidative phosphorylation and ATP production (energy production) within the mitochondria of all cells • one tablet (500 mg) per day

With this approach you will not empty out your wallet or overfill your medicine shelf. And speaking of the medicine shelf, it is important to note that vitamins and supplements should be stored away from children. The interesting, colorful capsules that are beneficial in small amounts can pose a hazard for children!

If the list of vitamins and supplements looks intimidating, it may be easiest to gradually build up the supplementation program. And if a lineup of capsules is simply too much to stomach in one sitting, you can distribute the supplementation over the day: one helping with breakfast and another with dinner. Most important is that you stay compliant. Haphazardly taking or forgetting the supplements will not do much for you. But consistently taking these high-potency supplements along with nutritious food will defend your body against the aging effect of free radicals.

How do vitamin and mineral supplements work?

Five major processes lead to premature aging: oxidant stress, inflammation, loss of mitochondrial function, insulin resistance, and loss of membrane integrity. There is a broad overlap of these various vitamins and minerals in terms of these processes, which ensures that the positive, supportive effects on the mitochondria and cell metabolism will prevent premature aging.

The following is a quick rundown of the uses of the various vitamins and minerals:

1. To fight oxidant stress: B vitamins (B_1, B_3, B_6, B_{12}, and folate), vitamin C, acetyl-L-carnitine, alpha-lipoic acid, bioflavonoid, garlic, ginger root extract, ginkgo biloba, ginseng, green tea extract, L-glutathione, magnesium, manganese, melatonin, N-acetyl cysteine, potassium, rutin, selenium, vitamin E, and coenzyme Q10
2. To fight inflammation: vitamin D, alpha-lipoic acid, bioflavonoid, garlic, ginger root extract, ginseng, green tea extract, melatonin, rutin, selenium, cod liver oil (omega-3), coenzyme Q10, and flaxseed oil
3. To preserve mitochondrial function: B vitamins (B_1, B_3, B_6, B_{12}, and folate), acetyl-L-carnitine, alpha-lipoic acid, ginger root extract, ginseng, selenium, and coenzyme Q10
4. To prevent insulin resistance: B vitamins (B_1, B_3, B_6, B_{12}, and folate), vitamin D, alpha-lipoic acid, beta-carotene, chromium picolinate, garlic, ginger root extract, ginseng, green tea extract, magnesium, manganese, potassium, and selenium
5. To provide membrane integrity: beta-carotene, garlic, ginger root extract, ginseng, selenium, cod liver oil (omega-3), and flaxseed oil

You can see that even when you take only part of the vitamins and minerals listed above, your body's integrity will still be protected.

Discuss supplementation and any questions surrounding the use of supplements with your health care provider before you embark on a program. Once you have decided to purchase supplements, read the labels carefully. Staff at health-food stores can also be a helpful source of information.

Cinnamon, an example of a spice that lowers heart attacks

Cinnamon has recently been found to have beneficial effects on the blood sugar, triglycerides, and LDL cholesterol levels of diabetics. Here is an article from one of my blogs where I reviewed this publication:

Cinnamon a natural insulin booster for diabetics

In a recent edition of the medical journal **Diabetes Care,** an interesting article appeared regarding the healing effect of the spice cinnamon. A medical research team in Pakistan (Khan, 2003) divided a group of sixty comparable diabetics aged between the ages of forty-five and fifty-five and fed one half different concentrations of cinnamon while the other half served as a placebo control. There were three different concentrations of capsules of cinnamon given: 1g, 3g, and 6g. The placebo group got capsules with inert material. Here are the results:

EFFECT OF CINNAMON ON BLOOD VALUES OF DIABETICS	
BLOOD COMPONENT INVESTIGATED	**REDUCTION OF BLOOD TEST**
Blood sugar level	18–29 %
Triglycerides (blood fat value)	23–30%
LDL cholesterol (damaging cholesterol)	7–27%
Total cholesterol	12–26%
HDL cholesterol (protective cholesterol)	unchanged

The control group showed no change in blood values. The effect documented in this table was achieved after forty days of cinnamon exposure and was "washed out" after twenty days. Other experiments have found that the substance MHCP (methylhydroxychalcone polymer) is the active ingredient in cinnamon that stimulates insulin and also acts on insulin receptors like insulin.

Dr. Richard A. Anderson and his colleagues at the Human Nutrition Research Center of the US Department of Agriculture had already published a number of medical papers on the effects of cinnamon. He was the coauthor of this study from the Department of Human Nutrition, NWFP Agricultural University of Peshawar, Pakistan.

The interesting observation here is that several cardiovascular risk factors (blood sugar, triglycerides, and LDL cholesterol) are simultaneously being reduced with something as simple as cinnamon powder. The authors stated that cinnamon oil is not effective, only cinnamon powder or a cinnamon stick dipped into tea (the water-soluble component of cinnamon). Dr. Anderson also warned not to eat more cinnamon buns or apple pie, as these contain unhealthy amounts of sugar, starch, and fat. He suggested that the best course of action would be to simply sprinkle cinnamon powder over whatever you are presently eating, as this will reduce the risk of diabetes or will reduce the risk of a heart attack in a diabetic individual.

The figures from this publication can be used as follows in a calculation of cardiovascular risk reduction. A moderate dose of cinnamon provides a reduction of 25 percent in blood sugar, 25 percent of triglycerides, and 15 percent of LDL cholesterol. If the probability of getting a heart attack for diabetics without cinnamon supplementation is set as 1.0, cinnamon supplementation would reduce this to 0.75 (blood sugar), 0.75 (triglycerides), and 0.85 (LDL cholesterol), provided there is a straight linear relationship. As all these beneficial effects occur simultaneously, the overall risk is even lower. It can be calculated by multiplying these separate risks, which results in an overall risk of only 0.48. This means that regular cinnamon supplementation can lead to a risk reduction of 52 percent, or about half of the risk compared to the placebo control group. And fortunately, cinnamon does not have any serious side effects, nor does it affect levels of the protective HDL cholesterol.

Vitamins and supplements including spices like curcumin and cinnamon help to stabilize cell metabolism. I have shown that many vitamins work by being anti-inflammatory, stabilizing mitochondria and cell membranes, fighting as anti-oxidants against free radicals and preventing insulin resistance. This supports all of the other modalities including lifestyle changes that are needed in concert to achieve a slowing down of the aging process.

Chapter 9:
Examining and Changing
Lifestyle Habits

Now that we know the significant risks associated with being obese and developing the metabolic syndrome, what can we do to modify or avoid such a risk?

Two major factors determine whether our weight stays the same or moves up or down: one is the net caloric intake of food (and drinks); the other is the caloric output from the average of our exercises. There are other factors of a metabolic nature—hypothyroidism, in which too little thyroid hormone is produced and the affected person does not burn enough calories, and hyperthyroidism, in which too much thyroid hormone production makes the person burn up a lot of extra calories—but caloric input and output are most influential. These two factors are essentially what determine how our bodies look. Add some food and take away some exercise, and you will register weight gain over several weeks and months. Remove the high-calorie snacks, stick to regular, balanced food intake, and couple this with a sensible exercise program, and your weight will come down to your ideal body weight and stay there.

Below I will explain in detail how to analyze your lifestyle, how it can be modified, and how you can maintain your modified lifestyle despite negative forces that may want to jeopardize your success. You can imagine that it is not as easy as it first sounds. To explain it better, I have broken it down into several segments below. Briefly I will explain why dieting alone does not work. I will explain why calorie restriction is necessary, but not by counting calories, but rather by changing your food intake to quality food intake where you remove the empty sugar and starch calories and increase your intake of vegetables and fruit. At the same time you are allowed healthy saturated fats and healthy omega-3 fats. To make it easier for you to change your food intake, I have included an appendix where my wife has provided seven days of nutritious breakfasts, lunches, dinners including desserts and snacks. Exercise is an important ingredient that cannot be missed. You need it seven days per week! So, let's start and review what you need to do.

A.) *Why dieting alone does not work in the long term*

Over the years I have seen many patients who started interesting diets, hoping to permanently lose weight. From a theoretical point of view, these diets are bound to fail because reactive hypoglycemia undermines the willpower of the dieter every one and a half to two hours. If we do not pay attention to our metabolic response to food changes, we run the risk of failure. You see, if we cut down the *quantity* of what we eat but still eat the same high-calorie, high refined-carbohydrate diet, we will create a powerful hypoglycemic reaction (low blood sugar level), which is bound to make us extremely hungry. This is the body's way of letting us know that we are changing our eating habits. Nature wants to keep everything stable, so cutting portions without improving the quality of what you eat will not work, as your metabolism will work against you.

Let me explain this in more detail. Refined carbohydrates are the foods like bread, cookies, sugar, french fries, chips, popcorn, and flour products. They are called "refined" because the food industry has processed them. Other unrefined high-glycemic carbohydrates are parsnips, potatoes, and dates; they contain a lot of starch or sugar naturally. When these foods are digested in the stomach, they are broken down very quickly into sugar and absorbed, bringing the blood sugar level up until it is cleared by an insulin response from the pancreas. One and a half to two hours later, the excess insulin lowers your blood sugar level to such an extent that you feel fierce hunger pangs again and are ready for your next carbohydrate-dense meal. The associated hunger pangs are too much to resist for many people, and this is why cutting down the quantity of food without changing the quality of the food intake will not work.

B.) *Calorie restriction*
Obesity is largely the end result of calorie mismanagement, in which the net balance is in favor of retaining excess calories. What happens to these extra calories? Your liver metabolizes the extra sugar into fatty acids, cholesterol, and triglycerides. Then your fatty tissue absorbs them, transforms them, and stores them as body fat. In the past there were famines from time to time, and people used these extra calories by melting the storage fat. This made sense back then, as the excess calories would be available for times when there was not enough food on the table. We all know that nowadays this rarely happens.

During the Second World War, heart attack rates in Germany went down dramatically because of general starvation. This shows that calorie restriction can be of some benefit. However, after the war was over, Germans experienced the *Wirtschaftswunder* (wonders of a thriving economy and affluence). This led to a high percentage of obesity associated with an alarming death rate from heart attacks and strokes in the late sixties and early seventies. All of this happened prior to the era of bypass surgeries and angioplasties, and almost every patient who was admitted to the hospital with a heart attack or stroke died! As an intern in German hospitals, I witnessed what was happening firsthand, and it appears to be happening again now on a large scale in the United States, Canada, and all the industrialized countries. Nobody knew back in the sixties that diabetes or high blood pressure was related to obesity through the metabolic syndrome. Nobody thought about prevention; it was the curative approach that ruled. We needed more hospital beds to "cure" all these people. Physicians then knew quite well that they could not really cure these patients with pills, procedures, or oxygen. Since then medicine has become more sophisticated, and this is good for those cases that benefit from it. However, when it comes to long-term solutions for the majority of obese patients, it is preventative weight loss with calorie management that is needed, not curative medicine and drugs. In other words, only prevention will make a long-term difference with regard to saving lives.

Managing excessive weight means to apply *calorie restriction*. Paying too much attention to diets and fitness can make you lose sight of this. Dr. Sears points out in his book *The Age-Free Zone* (Sears 2000) that calorie restriction is an integral part of any regime of prolonging life. The patients of the Framingham Heart Study who lost more than thirteen years of their lives over a span of forty years could have changed this by reducing smoking, restricting calories, adopting a well-balanced diet, and doing regular exercise. These patients would have lived thirteen years longer! Granted, everybody would have had to put an extra effort into this, as nothing is for free, but it is amazing how relatively simple and effective preventative risk reduction is.

This chapter describes an effective program that combines the right foods (including the low- to medium-GI carbs) with a regular exercise routine. It works because there are no hunger pangs (no hypoglycemic episodes), and there is a mild calorie restriction every day depending on how many low-calorie snacks you eat. There is no need to measure food by weighing or counting calories. All I am asking you to do is to step on the scale to monitor your daily weight. This should be recorded for about three months (in writing), just so you are tuned into yourself and keeping honest with what you want to achieve. After that time most people are disciplined enough that they do not have to write the weight down every day, although it is still the best measure of how you are doing with your weight-loss program (just between you and the scales).

C.) *The importance of an exercise program*

Fitness is part of a healthy lifestyle. It is a force to be reckoned with, yet the recognition of its importance is relatively new. Even in the last century, our ancestors could relate to sports, but *fitness* would have been a foreign term.

Our forefathers had a lot of physical activity built into their daily living. They had to work harder and walk a lot more, whereas we have the conveniences of public transportation and our own vehicles. Machines help us cope with previously heavy physical work, and we enjoy having more free time for our recreation. This all sounds very positive, but the advantages of our high-tech society can quickly become disadvantages.

We spend our free time sitting in front of computers and TVs; we sit in the car to drive to the movies. We drive to an arena and watch the physical workout of the hockey team, football team, soccer team, or baseball team. We actually may spend a morning or afternoon at a ball game, but not infrequently the beer and the hot dogs afterward counterbalance the benefit of this activity!

In a guilty attempt to be fit, we join a gym or health club, and we will go twice or three times per week. For one or two hours, we will work out and work up a sweat. The muscle aches after pumping weights tell us that we have been active indeed, and we believe that we have done something good for our health and fitness. No pain, no gain, and we are sore all over! So it must be true.

But is it really? In all likelihood the answer is no. We need physical exercise on an ongoing basis. Cramming an overdose that makes us good and sore for three days is not the answer. In chapter 5 I discussed a variety of different aspects of regular exercise, and you can review this again. The table below summarizes the importance of engaging in regular exercise rather than a one-time marathon that could kill you.

Regular exercise, not a deadly marathon!

The original marathon runner who arrived in the Greek capital of Athens to proclaim the victory of his army fell down dead after he had run the marathon. He likely was not carefully trained, he just ran as fast as he could, but he collapsed dead. This is not what we should do. Instead we need to be physically active, ideally every day of the week to condition our bodies to stay fit. This is not impossible: all we need is thirty-five minutes of a brisk walk. Strength training is also desirable. But your best bet is to do a regular exercise routine every day of the week, because this matches your metabolism that is active every day.

I like to work out for fifty-five to sixty minutes every day. I spend thirty minutes on a treadmill, spending about 300 calories. This is followed by twenty-five to thirty minutes of isometric exercises (weights, machines) for strength training; these are also called anaerobic exercises. Aerobic exercise is the other part of exercising—the treadmill, bicycle, or elliptical trainer. It is important for our cardiovascular fitness, and we can also meet this demand by brisk walking. It is not good enough to do only half an hour of weight lifting or half an hour of jogging. The success of an exercise program lies in the *balance* of the aerobic and the anaerobic exercise. Chapter 5 explained possible exercises (aerobic and anaerobic) in more detail.

Basic exercise plan

1. Aerobic exercise for 30 minutes

2. Upper and lower body strength training for 5 to 10 minutes each

If you want to create a more intense program, you can do the following:

Aerobic exercise (bicycle, treadmill, brisk power walk) that burns up 300 calories

Weight training at home or at the gym 3 times per week, but not exceeding 60 minutes

Some flexibility training: stretches, yoga, Pilates

Above is the basic program that I mentioned earlier in chapter 5. For your convenience I have reprinted it here.

D.) *Analyze your particular problem*

Let me review what we have learned so far. In the beginning of the book, I indicated that certain conditions are linked with the metabolic syndrome. The Framingham Heart Study in the United States has shown that obesity is the driving force that leads to most of the metabolic changes that cause premature death from heart attacks, strokes, and cancer. It also causes high blood pressure, infertility, arthritis and diabetes.

It is important to know at the beginning what your particular baseline is with respect to obesity-related clinical problems. This is where a physician can help you. An ECG would help to show whether there is a strain on your heart. Blood tests with HDL and LDL cholesterol subfractions would also be desirable. If you smoke, you should discuss with the doctor whether you will quit on your own or might need some help with a nicotine patch. Your body mass index should also be recorded. All of this will establish the baseline. You could possibly locate your particular risk mix on table 2 and with the help of figures 1 and 2. You might identify risks on table 1 and multiply the identified risk factors and calculate your risk. You should discuss this with your health care provider.

But all of this is not as important as actually doing the steps. This begins with choosing the right foods: low-to medium-GI foods and the right amount of good fats (as discussed in chapter 4). Further you want to combine this with the right amount of exercise as indicated in chapter 5, such as going for regular thirty-minute walks seven days a week (as a minimum), which will subtract about 300 calories per day (Sears, 2000). There is no magic to this. The magic is when you realize that you are actually more powerful than you thought you would be! You can still watch your favorite hockey game or football game on TV, but you should also get going by moving about. The scales will faithfully accompany you and quietly tell you the truth. Most of the time when the scales go up a pound, you will know why. Go back and think about it. If you have problems figuring it out, you may have to follow the more detailed method described below.

E.) *Determine your goal*

Even if your BMI is 35 or 40 (well into the obesity category), start somewhere. Do not be concerned about your goal. The higher the value is, though, the more important it is that you have a health professional supervise your weight-loss program. Between a BMI of 25 and 30 (overweight category), most people could likely manage this themselves. However, to ensure that there are no contraindications (meaning no health condition stands in the way), I would suggest that everybody check with a physician prior to embarking on such a program to get the OK to proceed.

Some may feel overpowered by the magnitude of the program, but there is no danger, no hunger pangs, and no metabolic problems because you are correcting the metabolic syndrome. The more you stick to the low- and medium-glycemic foods and the more vegetables, fruit, lean meat, and medium-fat cheeses you eat, the fewer hypoglycemic episodes you will experience. I found that within only two to three months of removing refined sugar completely from their food intake, patients discovered that the hypoglycemia episodes that had plagued them for years had disappeared for good. And why should they not disappear? When you remove the ingested sugar or the sugar as a byproduct of the breakdown from refined flour, white breads, white rice, pasta, or potatoes, you remove the stimulus to the pancreas to produce excessive insulin. This leads to a normalization of the blood sugar level, and you will lose the cravings for "comfort foods" (sugar and starches). Foggy thinking will become a thing of the past! By selecting the right foods from the low- to medium-GI foods as discussed in chapter 4 you will at the same time remove your food cravings.

Having said all of this, what should your goal be? A reasonable goal for your BMI would be in the range of 21 to 24. The reason I can say this is that the height and weight ratio averages most of the various body shapes and bone-density variations. However, if you have concerns about this, see your physician and ask what your particular BMI goal should be. It is my experience that you cannot fool your body and that you will eventually level off at the BMI that is ideal for you automatically. In other words, your body will guide you to your goal, which, again, will be within 21 to 24 for most people. There is a small but important group of patients with the conditions anorexia nervosa, bulimia, or binge eating disorder. They need to be supervised by a physician. Some of them may not be able to stop at their ideal BMI.

F.) *Get ready to change your food intake*
You have all the background material you need to change your lifestyle. I would invite you to simply choose your food more from the table on page 44 and avoid foods from the table on page 42. You will notice that by doing this you will automatically cut out unhealthy fats, because you will avoid the trans fatty acids (hydrogenated or partially hydrogenated fats). If you are ready, go ahead and do this.

Others may want to implement this change more methodically by first keeping a dietary log for perhaps one week. This can be done as follows:

- Write everything down that you eat or drink with estimates of quantities.
- Circle all the foods that belong into the table on page 42 (best in red). Your goal is to remove these from your acceptable-food list.
- Take your weight on a daily basis, first thing in the morning (always at about the same time), and record this on your food list or on a separate sheet of paper to which you can refer back, in case this is necessary.
- Determine your BMI by weighing yourself and measuring your height. This website can help you to calculate it easier: http://nhlbisupport.com/bmi/bminojs.htm

Armed with this knowledge, you have established a baseline for your BMI. You have also established your baseline weight. With the help of your food list, you can analyze whether or not there is a problem and pinpoint it to the exact food that you have circled in red that you must remove from now on.

I find that the food list used in this manner is a very powerful tool for those who like to be rational about what they are doing (linear thinkers). However, if you are more the type who goes by your gut feeling and can't be bothered about numbers, do not despair. You can choose the foods from the table on page 44 and eat until you are no longer hungry and be guided by your daily weights (I know, there is still a number on the scales, but that's different).

Taking your daily weight is one of the rules that all have to abide by. I do this for myself even years after having changed to a well-balanced food intake. I do it because it keeps me honest, and I would notice right away if I gained weight. I can also see that my regular exercise program works, and I can measure the effect of any dietary indiscretion.

Here I'd like to review the basics of the sensible food intake again. It starts with **breakfast** in the morning, as outlined in chapter 4. Good nutrition involves three meals, namely breakfast, lunch, and dinner. In between you can eat snacks. Studies have shown that when you have more than only two or three meals a day, the production of the digestive juices requires more internal consumption of energy, helping your goal of weight reduction (it's like getting a freebie).

Note that protein portions are always roughly measured by the size of the palm of your hand. The rest is fruit or vegetables from the list of low- to medium-glycemic foods (see table on page 44) or the website with a more complete listing of foods and their glycemic indices. If you do not have access to the Internet, ask your friends to give you a printout of the various food groups for your fridge. While you're at it, ask them to make some extra copies for mutual friends and for themselves. Invariably this gets conversations going, and it is better when these are based on facts.

My previous remarks regarding junk meats is important (chapter 4). I take the sausage story so serious that I will not eat sausage anymore. It contains unnecessary and unhealthy fat, leftovers of lower-quality meat (covered up by spicing), and nitrites and nitrates for preservation. It's a deadly mix that can attack your arteries and cause cancer and it will cause a weight problem. Keep the fat facts in mind as already mentioned. As a source of omega-3 fatty acids, which we all need for our brains and natural steroid hormones, I recommend supplementation with two to three capsules of fish oil as mentioned in chapter 8. However, if you eat salmon or mackerel three times per week and coarse oats for breakfast, you likely will get enough omega-3 fatty acids even without supplements. Bear in mind that omega-3 fatty acids in fish oil are beneficial not only to your general well-being, but also to your cardiovascular health and reduction or prevention of inflammation. For these reasons alone, you should consider taking these supplements!

Cottage cheese, a few slices of skim-milk mozzarella cheese (15 percent fat), or provolone cheese (up to 25 percent) will be good snacks. Read labels, and don't be shy about asking if the label is not visible at the deli counter. A good breakfast would be a spinach omelet and a coup of coffee sweetened with stevia.

Lunch suggestions are given in chapter 4 and the appendix. The biggest surprise is the absence of bread, potatoes, and pasta. You do not need them. The inhabitants of Okinawa do not need those foods, and they have the most and the healthiest centenarians on earth! Like them, we can eat more vegetables and more salads. You may want to order Japanese at the food court of your favorite shopping mall, such as a stir-fry with vegetables, but skip the rice. Some green tea with stevia (you probably have to bring your stevia along) would go very nicely with this. Plain yogurt with a piece of fruit could be a dessert or a snack in between lunch and dinner (watch for calorie content of yogurt, and make sure the product does not contain a fruit-sugar mixture.)

When dinner comes along, the important principles are to stay away from bread and other starchy foods, as explained with lunch. A good portion of lean meat or fish will satisfy your appetite (again, size the portion of meat according to the size of the palm your hand). Stick to the principles that I outlined in chapter 4 regarding food intake. We need to feed our machinery the right fuel, or it will not run as many miles.

Citation from "The Okinawa Program"

"Our study found the elders to have incredibly young arteries, low risk for heart disease and stroke, low risk for hormone-dependent cancers (healthy breasts, ovaries, prostates, and colons), strong bones, sharp minds, slim bodies, natural menopause, healthy levels of sex hormones, low stress levels, and excellent psychospiritual health. Okinawans who follow the traditional lifestyle are simply very healthy people. There is obviously a great deal to learn from them". Source: Willcox, 2001 (chapter 1, page 9)

This quotation reminds us that the Okinawans do not live to an old age by chance (Willcox, 2001). It is not a genetic advantage that they have; in fact, young Okinawans who move away and change their ways of eating get the same diseases as those of the host country they live in and die prematurely. But those who hold on to the traditional foods and ways of the Okinawans turn centenarians in the host country. This is good news for us, as it suggests that this plan will work anywhere in the world.

In the last chapter of this book, you will find an appendix with a few recipes to get you started. It shows you that a sensible food intake (I prefer this expression instead of calling it the Okinawa Program or the Zone diet) is not boring, tastes interesting, and keeps you energetic although your BMI stays in the desirable range (normal weight for height).

Some people may wonder when to "stop the diet." My answer to this is that there is no diet: you have just adopted a healthy food-intake pattern. There is no beginning and no end. It is ongoing. It is healthy. It is the reason your metabolic syndrome will never come back: you will use the same healthy, low-glycemic food intake as maintenance. When people on the Okinawa Islands are following their native diet, nobody asks them, "And when do you get off your diet?" They simply live their lives taking in a low-glycemic diet the way they have always done. Mediterranean people like the Greeks and Italians in the country setting who eat vegetables and fruit also practice a low-glycemic food intake. The only problem is that modern civilization, with the sugar and candy overload and powerful images from TV commercials, is undermining this practice, and a shift from low and medium glycemic foods to high-glycemic foods is taking place. It is time to reclaim healthy eating habits and do the opposite!

The next three subsections are meant as a safeguard against forces that may attempt to undermine your willpower.

G.) *Have emotional backup on stand-by*
Many of you will find that there are all kinds of people around you who will attempt to undermine your decision to change your eating habits and your lifestyle. It is important, therefore, to surround yourself

with a network of support. I would hope that your marital partner (or boyfriend/girlfriend) would be supportive. If not, discuss your intentions and the rationale. With reasoning and patience—and seeing the first results of your lifestyle changes—this support will hopefully come. Often it takes some time for people around us to get used to our new body image. Some people perceive it as a threat when their friends suddenly lose forty or fifty pounds, as they perceive pressure to do the same. If they are not ready to do this, they may get frustrated and put you down, as this is easier than changing their own ways.

Other support systems include groups like Weight Watchers or Tops. Here is a URL that links to a list of support groups on the Internet: http://www.dmoz.org/Health/Weight_Loss/Support_Groups/

H.) *Start your program and stick to it*

In the end it is *your* decision what you would like to do. I cannot talk you into it. Your friends cannot talk you into it. The question is what you want out of life. I would suggest that you think about what I wrote in this book. Listen around. Read other books. Read more about the metabolic syndrome or about the various publications of the ongoing Framingham Heart Study. Read some of the reference material cited at the end of this book. You will find that the science around the metabolic syndrome is solid. It is a fundamental new discovery in modern medicine that weaves itself like a red thread through all of the medical fields. It touches on literally every disease process in medicine, and many physicians are beginning to rethink what they were taught in medical school.

The pathology of the disease processes has not changed, but the pathophysiological thinking and interpretation of it has changed dramatically over the years in light of the newer research. Cancer, arthritis, high blood pressure, heart attacks, strokes, diabetes, and obesity are all connected to the metabolic syndrome. Risk factors as depicted in tables 1 and 2 or in Fig. 1 and 2 can now be turned around through lifestyle intervention. You can have a profound impact on whether you want to age in dignity and stay vibrant for as long as possible or whether you want to spend your golden years prematurely aged due to disabilities. Change never comes easy. However, the rewards of aging without major disabilities are well worth it.

You will meet people who tell you, "I don't want to live forever." I am not promising that you will. Nobody does! But you will improve your chances of aging slower and staying healthier for longer. Genetically we all have our limits—some in our eighties, some in our nineties—but with the Okinawa-type lifestyle, which is close to what I have described in this book, the genetic limit may be pushed to reach one hundred, all the while staying well and retaining our physical and mental functions. The epigenetic factors of the environment that we are changing automatically switch positive gene switches in our DNA on and negative gene switches off. Enjoy the energy that comes from a combination of a brisk walking program seven days a week (or a regular gym program), a change to the balanced-fat, low-glycemic food intake as described in chapter 4 and a relaxation program that you pursue every day for a short time (described in chapter 6). It becomes a new routine within about two to three months. It is easier to adopt and to stick to than you may think.

I.) *Withstand seductions that want to throw you off your program*

What should you do if you pigged out on a holiday and found yourself back to your old food habits with high carbs? Don't panic. Stop any self-accusations; they do not serve you well. Instead, think of it as a mistake, and move on. Start taking in protein snacks and lean cheese snacks instead of high-carb snacks. Also choose your foods from the table on page 44 and emphasize the foods with the lower glycemic index (mostly below 55 percent). This will allow you to regain control over the sugar-induced hypoglycemia spells. Be aware that it could take two to six weeks before you are back on track. It takes that long for your hormone changes to normalize and for your psyche to feel at ease again. Think of it as a learning experience. You probably felt lousy because of a lack of energy, sluggishness, and a lack of motivation to do your regular exercise program. When you feel your energy return, when your emotions are on an even keel again, and when your weight is moving toward your ideal BMI again, you will know deep inside that this is good for you.

Remember that only you can choose which way you live. If you decide to follow a balanced-fat, low-glycemic food intake, you will find coping mechanisms that defend you from any food seductions around you, and your daily weights will remind you what you want to eat and what you don't. After you've made a mistake, you can start again with the healthy choices you learned before.

Chapter 10:
Monitoring Your Lifestyle Choices

Any successful businessperson knows how important it is to monitor a company's progress. We humans are our own managers. As you grow up, your parents may or may not tell you what you should eat. Eventually we are our own food bosses. Some people find it easy to stick to certain food choices such as those suggested in this book. Others may need reminders. The best reminder is your daily weight. If it is going in an up or down direction, it would be wise to record it somewhere where you can easily retrieve it so that you can think about its direction when one week has passed. If it goes back up into the direction where you came from (in the case of obesity), you may want to record all of your food (and drink) intake. This way you could, if needed, calculate your exact calorie intake per day. I agree, though, that this is no fun and is much too laborious. It is much simpler to identify the food components and whether or not they are contained on the table of high-GI foods mentioned in chapter 4. They may not be listed in the case of cakes, pies, white rice, or pasta, or they may have a slightly different name. This table is only to remind you that starchy foods and foods processed with white flour or starch all belong in the category of high-GI foods. However, with the help of your scales, you can figure this out. Remember that for years you likely never paid much attention to these energy issues. This means that you can now take your time to find a way that works for you and is palatable for you (no pun intended).

Do not forget to incorporate active exercises such as a brisk thirty- to forty-five-minute walk every day or the equivalent for calorie expenditure. Such a small change will use up to 300 calories per day or 2,100 calories per week! It is a painless way to lose pounds easily.

The purpose of monitoring your progress is to ensure that the metabolic changes of the metabolic syndrome are being changed into a balanced metabolism. We recognize progress by experiencing weight loss down to a normal BMI (ranging between 21 and 24). We also see this from the daily weights and the direction in which we are slowly moving. We can monitor our food intake and compare it with the low- to medium-GI food list. Is our food intake compatible? We also know that if we engage in regular physical exercise of our choosing, we will burn additional calories, and the internal hormonal changes toward metabolic stabilization will begin to take place automatically.

Chapter 11:
Results of Your Lifestyle Changes and the Future

As already indicated, making lifestyle changes means removing some of the risk factors listed above. Let us deal with this situation briefly here. With regular exercise, the good cholesterol (HDL) will come up to normal levels. You will remember from chapter 2 that this reduces the risk for dying from a heart attack from around 23-fold (group 4 in table 2 and Fig.1) to a risk of 14- to 16-fold (group 3). When elevated blood pressure is treated aggressively with antihypertensive medication, the ECG strain will disappear, particularly when the cardiac load is reduced as well by reducing body weight through the sensible food intake discussed above. This will reduce the risk to develop a heart attack over the next sixteen years to 6.2- to 8.43-fold (group 2 in table 2 and Fig.1). Next diabetes can be controlled by a low-GI diet and other measures with the help of a physician. This will reduce the risk to 3.2- to 4.6-fold (group1 in table 2 and Fig. 1). We are now only left with the risks due to obesity and smoking. With the diet changes (cutting out sugar and starches) a lot of weight has come off, so that the risk from obesity will have disappeared the moment the BMI is below 25.0. The risk of developing a heart attack in the next 16 sixteen years is now down to 1.93- to 2.78-fold, and is from the remaining risk of smoking. Once the person also quits smoking and keeps the weight below a BMI of 25.0, the risk will be down to "none," meaning that the risk now is that of the control group (which is the background population with no risk factors).

I use this example to demonstrate the principle of *risk intervention*. You and your physician know your own risk setting. You can set goals for yourself and work on improving your life expectancy. Remember figure 2, where over forty years and involving only two risks (obesity and smoking) thirteen years were lost for this patient group in the Framingham Heart Study. Why let this happen? Why not turn it around by quitting smoking and by losing weight without hunger pangs?

I like you to briefly take a look at the image on the cover of this book. The first segment of the pie diagram shows the average life expectancy of up to 80 years. This would involve quitting smoking, drinking minor to moderate amounts of alcoholic beverages, doing some exercises and activities; some people will have had joint replacements for arthritis and stents for narrowed coronary arteries. This is about the limit of what conventional medicine can do for you. The second segment of the pie diagram indicates a life expectancy of between 80 and 100 years. These people may have better genetics, but they likely are also those who drink less and never smoked or have given up smoking decades ago. Their body weight will be in the ideal body mass index range or in the only slightly overweight range. They exercise fairly regularly, although not too conscientiously.

The third segment of the pie diagram (between the ages of 100 and 120) requires more effort on your part. To achieve that additional life expectancy you need to take the quality of your food intake seriously and stick to mostly organic foods. Regular foods from grocery stores are so contaminated with chemicals and toxins and full of GMO foods that it would not support your body to such a ripe old age; hence the recommendation to eat mostly organic foods. In order to have full body functions you need to replace missing hormones with bioidentical ones and have hormone levels checked from time to time. As we learnt from chapter 8 just adding multiple vitamins and supplements will give you more than 9 years of additional lifetime because of telomere lengthening. Regular exercise is needed as well to keep the circulation going so that oxygen and nutrients reach every body cell. If you follow the recommendations in this book, your body mass index will be well below 25.0, more likely in the 21 to 23 range. Your chance of entering into this group of life expectancy is very good. As you concentrate on prevention, you will have no aches and pains, no arthritis and likely no disabilities or dementia.

The choice of how you live your life is yours. If you choose to cut out only a few risk factors, the Framingham Heart Study has shown that your life expectancy will go up significantly. The newer knowledge about this is that a change in dietary habits combined with a moderate exercise program and a simple relaxation method can bring your hormones back into balance. In this balanced state, your arteries do not get clogged as easily and may actually reopen again in some areas. With your weight down to your ideal body mass index (21 to 24), you will have more energy, and your sex life will likely be more satisfying. Women who were infertile before might have normal hormone cycles again and achieve pregnancy more easily. Medical conditions such as diabetes, high blood pressure, arthritis, and autoimmune diseases will be easier to control by your physician or may even normalize on their own. The reason behind this is that the immune system will stop being in alarm mode. With significant weight loss, the insulin levels tend to normalize in patients with type 2 diabetes, and the insulin receptors begin responding normally again. The omega-3 fatty acids, which are often lacking in adequate amounts in a high-glycemic/low-fat diet, will be present again. This leads to profound hormone rebalancing as well as a normalization of the brain metabolism. The end result is a renewed surge of energy. Your memory will improve as well, and you will have a sense of general well-being.

The future is already there in the Okinawa population that adheres to the original well-balanced eating habits (Willcox, 2001). But as the authors of this reference point out, the Okinawa subpopulation that has adopted Western eating habits (high-glycemic foods and high unhealthy fat content) has a shorter life span. Not surprisingly the result of this is an increase in all of the known diseases of the Western society, such as heart attacks, strokes, cancer, and arthritis. It follows from this that it is up to us to choose the right way to live if we want to enjoy life to the fullest and stay mobile for as long as possible.

Finally, let us not forget the emotional aspect of our lives. We need close contact with friends in an atmosphere of trust and love. Negative feelings need to be dealt with. We can do this in a variety of ways, such as talking to a close friend or a spouse. If family support is not available, support groups may be needed. Religious groups that are life affirming and positive can provide a network of social support and a source of faith and confidence. This enables people to cope with difficult life circumstances. Prayer and meditation in a religious context reduce the stress response that filters down from the brain into the hypothalamus, the pituitary gland, and the adrenal glands. The end result is a much lower ACTH response from the pituitary gland and a much lower cortisol level from the adrenal glands in the blood. This in turn strengthens the immune cells and provides resistance against serious viral infections. Susceptibility to the flu, which is one of the deadly consequences of aging in the Western world, is no longer as big a problem (nevertheless, I would still recommend the yearly flu injection). One word of caution: ask for a flu serum, which is mercury free. It should not contain thimerosal!

Your golden years are not a matter of chance. Despite the long-standing belief that disabilities in old age are inevitable, newer medical research shows that this is not the case. Biologically it is feasible to live longer and healthier, but you need to take charge of your life at least in the midforties or early fifties to make a difference in your later years. The sooner you adopt the lifestyle described in this book, the more you benefit. Contrary to many people's belief, this can be achieved without any extra costs, without costly memberships at gyms or weight-reduction clinics. It can be done at home. The key is prevention. This is not curative medicine, but preventative medicine.

Eventually you may forget that you read this and simply start to believe that you had that thought yourself to take charge of your life, eat the right things, get physically more fit, and relax more. It doesn't sound complicated. You will recognize that this really is all common sense. You probably thought of a healthy lifestyle and had similar ideas. Now you see it all in print, and it's your personal lifestyle program for health and vibrancy. You are embracing it! Congratulations!

Appendix:
Successful Aging in the Kitchen

by Christina Schilling

One week of recipes for breakfast, lunch, and dinner (dessert and snacks included)

For some people the idea of cooking may be intimidating. It's not. For starters, forget the idea that you have to enroll in cooking classes in order to be an accomplished chef. At its most basic, cooking is nothing more than a survival skill. It doesn't have to be challenging or boring. You can find your own personal style so it can be a creative and fun activity that gives you a good deal of satisfaction. We have become too used to having everything prepackaged and precooked, all ready to go in a zip-open-and-warm-up package; all you need is a driver's license to take a trip to the next drive-through restaurant or takeout place. At this point the definition of good food becomes rather foggy. You have to ask yourself whether food that is very often overprocessed is the quality fuel that your body deserves and whether it is the best choice for family members, friends, or guests.

It is a good idea to reassess the conventional pantry and the staples you need. Pick a quiet, undisturbed stretch of time to take a close look at your storage and start weeding out. You may be shocked at the number of nutritionally empty items you have housed there. If you really consider the fact that potato chips, pretzels, popcorn, and instant pudding are nutri-garbage that doesn't do you or your family any good, you will find it easy to sink the whole lot into a garbage bag. You may find that your pantry looks empty once you have ditched all the questionable cans, packages, and bags—the crackers, cookies, cereal boxes, and pasta packages. You may even have space for your food processor or blender once the ten-pound bags of rice, flour, and sugar have disappeared from the shelves! You may enjoy a Crock-pot (slow cooker), which is great for having dinner ready when you come home in the evening. It also makes it possible to turn less- expensive cuts of meat into great meals that pack a lot of flavor. Three items that can be your most valuable allies are a wok with a high-quality nonstick surface, a nonstick frying pan (reserved for omelets or frittatas), and an electric griddle/grill. I find that the wok is my most frequently used item for cooking.

As far as grocery shopping is concerned, you know already that most of the valuable food choices are located at the periphery of the supermarket. As a result you will shop for fresh food: meats, fish, vegetables, fruit, and some dairy choices like yogurt (if you desire). Again, it is important to choose organic dairy products, as many large commercial dairies process milk from cows that have been treated with bovine growth hormone to increase their milk production. This highly controversial hormone is already prohibited in Canada and in Europe. Some people who are sensitive to cow's milk find that goat's milk is the better choice for them. And if it's just the glass of milk that is dear to you, almond milk is a good fit. Keep in mind, though, that while it is lower in fat, as a protein source, almond milk is not a good choice, as it contains only very low amounts.

You will need enough room in your fridge for food storage. Plastic Ziploc bags are useful for storing greens. Also look out for vegetable storage bags. Some plastic or glass containers with lids are a practical

addition for storing almonds or other nuts. Keeping them refrigerated prevents them from turning rancid. You will also use your freezer
space, especially for meats. Deep-frozen vegetables and berries can
be an economical choice, as long as you are choosing organically
grown products. But stay away from the creamed spinach or the corn
in butter sauce. These products have added ingredients (usually fat
and flour) that you should avoid. As you shop, pick up a bottle of
extra-virgin organic olive oil. Some individuals like coconut oil. It has
become a popular choice, and an organic product can be useful if you
cook or panfry with high temperatures. I avoid cooking with high temperatures and cook with olive oil. The oils to avoid are those rich in
omega-6 fatty acids: sunflower oil, safflower oil, grape-seed oil, soy-
bean oil, and corn oil. The latter two are open to even more scrutiny,
as both corn and soy are commonly genetically modified.

You will certainly want to explore the great world of herbs and
spices—they are wonderful for giving food a new twist. But read the
labels before you consider spice mixes. Many of them contain flavor
enhancers. Very often the label on a seasoning mix says "natural flavors," which is commonly an expression for monosodium glutamate
(MSG), a known excitotoxin—a substance that destroys brain cells.
Fresh parsley, basil, cilantro, or thyme, just to name a few, are great
herbs to use in salad dressings or marinades. And they certainly need
no flavor enhancers. To add sweetness to a dessert, a product like
powdered stevia or a bottle of vanilla stevia will be handy. Sugar is
not something you should be using. No sugar—whether it is natural,
brown, or organic—is desirable. Beware of honey, too. "Healthy" honey
will produce as much of an unhealthy insulin spike as maple syrup or
the currently fashionable agave syrup. The latter has similar undesirable qualities to high fructose corn syrup! For the preparation of salad
dressings, you may like a bottle of balsamic vinegar. If you do not want
the dark color of balsamic, light balsamic vinegar is available. And you
can experiment with other vinegars. Red wine vinegar, apple cider vinegar, rice vinegar—it is all about your personal preferences. Another
flavorful option is fresh lemon juice. So keeping a few organic lemons

in the fridge is no mistake, as the grated peel gives a Mediterranean spin to Greek-style marinated meats or adds a sunny, fresh taste to a smoothie. Mineral water with fresh-squeezed lemon juice and a small amount of stevia is also a very refreshing beverage.

You will find all the ingredients for healthy cooking in a well-stocked supermarket. For more organic choices, you will have to take a stroll through a local health food store. Farmers' markets often offer seasonal organically produced fruit and vegetables. Frequently these markets are held on weekends and make for a nice outing, provided you have one close to your home. In more rural areas, you have the ability to inquire with local farmers. Shopping does not have to be overwhelming, but it is of great help if you get to know to your stores and thus prevent time-consuming shopping trips. Have your list ready, and do not go on your shopping expedition with an empty stomach; otherwise, you may be tempted to buy on impulse. Save yourself money, and stick to your original list! If you are out shopping with your kids, it's a good idea to feed them before you head out, or else they may discover every useless candy bar special for you and will try to "help" put items you originally did not want to buy into your shopping cart! And now for some food choices that will see you through the day with an emphasis on easy preparation!

Breakfast

Often breakfast is the most neglected meal of the day. It does not have to be, as advance preparation helps to avoid a narrow passage in the kitchen!

Gluten-Free Muesli

(2 servings)

⅔ cup of quinoa flakes*

1 tablespoon chopped almonds

1 tablespoon pumpkin seeds

1 tablespoon ground flax seeds

1 tablespoon sunflower seeds

1 tablespoon whole psyllium husk (optional)

1 scoop of protein powder (vegan or egg-white protein)

1½ cups almond milk

Stevia or stevia-vanilla, according to taste

Fresh fruit: 1½ cups of mixed berries (fresh or frozen and defrosted) or one apple (diced)

Combine dry ingredients in a bowl. (To save time, prepare them the evening before). Stir in the almond milk, and add the sweetener. Let stand for 10 minutes. Divide into 2 helpings. Add more almond milk if desired, and top with fresh fruit. You may enjoy a sprinkle of cinnamon over the muesli.

*For individuals who are not affected by celiac disease, the same quantity of old-fashioned rolled oats (not fast-cooking or instant) can be used.

Super Vegetable Scramble

(2 servings)

½ chopped green pepper

½ cup chopped green onions

½ cup sliced fresh mushrooms (white or crimini)

½ cup chopped yellow or green zucchini

1 tablespoon olive oil or coconut oil

2 eggs

4 egg whites (or ¾ cup liquid egg whites)

½ teaspoon salt

Sprinkle of freshly ground pepper

2 tablespoons crumbled goat cheese

½ avocado, sliced

1 tomato, sliced

Prepare the vegetables and set aside. This can be done the evening before.

In a mixing bowl, stir eggs, egg whites, salt, and pepper. In nonstick frying pan, heat the oil. Add the prepared vegetables, and sauté at medium heat. Add the egg mixture. Scramble once the eggs start to set. Sprinkle with the crumbled goat cheese. Distribute the vegetable-egg scramble on 2 plates. Garnish with avocado and tomato slices.

Baked Quinoa Custard

(2 servings)

⅔ cup quinoa

1½ cups water

Pinch of salt

1 cup almond milk

2 eggs and 1 egg white

1 teaspoon vanilla extract

Stevia to taste

½ teaspoon of grated lemon peel (optional)

2 tablespoons slivered almonds

1 apple, cored and sliced

Bring water and salt to a boil, and add quinoa. Cover and let cook for 15 minutes or until quinoa is soft. Remove from heat and fluff with a fork. (Can be prepared the evening before.) In mixing bowl beat eggs and egg whites; add almond milk, stevia, lemon peel, and slivered almonds. Put mixture into oiled ovenproof bowl. Place into microwave and cook at high power for 10 minutes till custard is firm. It can also be cooked in individual serving bowls. Top with apple slices and serve.

Great Greens Omelet

(2 servings)

1 tablespoon olive oil or coconut oil

3 chopped green onions

3 cups spinach leaves or a mix of greens: kale, spinach, Swiss chard

1 red pepper, cut into strips

3 eggs and 3 egg whites

2 tablespoons grated parmigiano

In nonstick pan sauté green onion, greens, and pepper strips in oil. Stir eggs and egg whites, and pour over the vegetables. Sprinkle with parmigiano. Cook on medium heat till the egg mixture starts to set. Turn over and briefly let cook. Remove from pan, divide into 2 portions, and sprinkle with a bit of salt (optional). Serve with salsa and guacamole.

For finicky kids that don't want to eat, give them something liquid! This also works for adults who are used to just downing a cup of coffee!

Rush Hour Breakfast Smoothie

(2 servings)

1 cup organic yogurt (not reduced fat)

¾ cup almond milk

1 tablespoon chia seeds

2 tablespoons almond butter

1 tablespoon protein powder

1½ cups strawberries or deep-frozen berry mix

Stevia or stevia vanilla according to taste

Variation: instead of berries use ½ apple and a peeled orange.

Put all ingredients into a blender jar and process till the mixture is smooth. Can be consumed immediately or taken along in a thermos.

No Grain Pancakes

(2 servings)

2 eggs and 2 egg whites

½ cup organic yogurt (cow's milk or goat's milk)

½ cup almond flour

1 tablespoon psyllium husk

1 tablespoon olive oil or coconut oil

2–3 teaspoons xylitol

Sprinkle of cinnamon

1½ cups blueberries

Stir together egg, egg whites, yogurt, almond flour, and psyllium husk. Preheat griddle or heat oil in nonstick pan. Pour small portions of batter onto grill or alternatively make larger pancakes. Bake at medium heat till golden, then turn over and bake the other side. Put on plates, sprinkle with xylitol and a bit of cinnamon, and serve with blueberries (fresh or defrosted previously frozen fruit).

Crustless Spinach Quiche

(4 servings)

6 eggs

4 egg whites

½ cup milk or light cream

¾ cup of shredded Swiss cheese or Gruyère

6 slices of back bacon, chopped into bits

Salt and pepper to taste

1 tablespoon olive oil

1 chopped onion

5 cups spinach leaves

Preheat oven to 375°F. In mixing bowl stir together the eggs, egg white, milk or cream, and salt and pepper. In frying pan or wok, sauté the spinach leaves and the onion in olive oil until the spinach leaves are wilted. Cool slightly, and stir the sautéed vegetables, chopped bacon, and shredded cheese into the egg mix. Grease a pie pan (glass or ceramic makes for easier serving). Pour the prepared vegetable and egg mixture into the prepared pie pan. Let the quiche bake at 375°F until the surface is golden brown and the quiche is set. If the top is browning too early, shield it with a piece of aluminum foil. Remove from oven, and serve warm.

A bowl of a colorful mixed fruit salad on the side completes this Sunday breakfast or brunch choice. The quiche can also be prepared ahead and reheated, which is a time-saver for busy week days.

Lunch

Lunch is a meal that is not often consumed leisurely. A lunch break at work can offer some time for socializing or going for a walk, but frequently we have no more than a few minutes for lunch. The worst lunch choice is getting a hamburger or hot dog from the food cart next door and wolfing it down in two minutes flat. The ready-made deli sandwich with mayo and ketchup is considered something to eat, but it does not provide you with good nutrition for the afternoon. Eating out and getting inferior food is neither a recipe for good health nor a sensible budgeting choice. If money is no object, you can get well-prepared lunch choices at a whole foods store or a health food store: pick a protein choice and a vegetable choice and enjoy! In real life this approach will set you back a few thousand dollars per year, money you would probably love to save for a trip! To get quality you can trust, you can prepare a bagged lunch. A container with salad greens and cut-up vegetables with a protein source, some fat (from olive oil, olives, or nuts), and some cut-up fruit for dessert can be a very tasty choice. Leftovers from a previous dinner are fine, too, if you can heat the meal up at your workplace. Packed lunches come to the rescue as well should you go on a road trip. You can stop chasing restaurants if you plan ahead; have a leakproof plastic container packed with good food and maybe a small thermos. It's that easy!

Lunch at home requires less planning ahead. On a weekend you may want to fix several helpings so you have some portable choices ready to take along during the week. The following recipe choices place emphasis on preparation in advance. They also do not require any reheating, so it's easy to pack them up for lunch. By the same token, you can make larger quantities for a picnic or a potluck.

Greek Salad To Go

(1 serving)

In a leakproof plastic container, put the following in layers:

1 cup cut-up romaine lettuce

1½ sliced tomatoes

¼ cup thinly sliced sweet onion

1 cup sliced cucumber

10 black olives

2 tablespoons crumbled feta cheese

Dressing

1½ tablespoons olive oil

1½ tablespoons light balsamic vinegar

Pinch of salt

1 teaspoon dried mixed Mediterranean herbs (oregano, basil, sage, rosemary)

Stir ingredients together, and pour over the salad. For additional protein top the salad with one hard-boiled egg or 3 ounces roasted chicken or turkey breast.

Lunch Spinach Salad

(1 serving)

2 cups baby spinach leaves

2 tablespoons sliced onion

3 tablespoons blue cheese (or use other choices: brie, camembert, cubed Swiss)

2 tablespoons walnuts or slivered almonds

2 hard-boiled eggs

1 tablespoon dried sour cherries or cranberries

Dressing

1½ tablespoons dark balsamic vinegar

1½ tablespoons olive oil

Pinch of salt

Layer all ingredients in bowl, finishing with the sliced or halved eggs. Stir together oil, vinegar, and salt, and pour over salad. Use leakproof, BPA-free container for lunch on the go.

Oriental Salad

(2 servings)

1 small sui choy cabbage (napa cabbage)

2 cups mung bean sprouts

1 small daikon radish, shredded to yield 1 cup

1 red pepper, cut into thin slices

3 green onions, chopped

1 medium carrot, cut into matchstick-size pieces

1 can sliced water chestnuts, rinsed

Dressing

2 tablespoons sesame oil

2 tablespoons rice vinegar (light balsamic vinegar works, too)

1 tablespoon tamari soy sauce

1 tablespoon Thai sweet chili sauce

1 teaspoon freshly grated ginger

3 tablespoons fresh cilantro, chopped

Prepare all vegetables, and put into salad bowl. Stir all dressing ingredients together, and pour over vegetable mix. Stir gently, cover, and refrigerate.

This salad can be consumed immediately or kept in the fridge for a day. To complete the salad with a protein portion, add your choice of 6 ounces cooked shrimp or the same quantity of cubed or sliced grilled chicken.

Stuffed Tomatoes

(2 servings)

3 large tomatoes

1 hard-boiled egg, sliced

6 ounces roasted chicken breast, chopped

3 tablespoons mayonnaise

3 teaspoons capers (or chopped pickles)

2 tablespoons chopped red pepper

3 cups baby lettuce leaves

1 tablespoon balsamic vinegar or lemon juice

Halve tomatoes and remove the seeds. In small mixing bowl, stir together the chopped chicken breast, mayonnaise, capers, and red pepper. Line a serving plate with lettuce, and sprinkle with balsamic vinegar or lemon juice. Spoon the prepared stuffing into the tomatoes and distribute any leftover stuffing on the lettuce. Place tomatoes on the lettuce bed, and decorate with egg slices.

Salad Rolls

(2 servings)

1 small head iceberg lettuce

1 package shirataki noodles, rinsed in boiling water*

8 ounces shrimp, chopped

3 green onions, chopped

1 carrot shredded or cut into julienne strips (thin strips)

1 can of sliced bamboo shoots, drained

3 tablespoons chopped cilantro leaves

1 teaspoon finely grated fresh ginger

2 tablespoons soy sauce

1 tablespoons hoisin sauce

2 tablespoons sesame oil

1 tablespoon lime juice

2 teaspoons sesame seeds

Loosen lettuce leaves from the head of lettuce, rinse, and pat dry. You should get about 6 to 8 large leaves. Put the prepared shirataki noodles, vegetables, and shrimp into a bowl. Add cilantro, ginger, soy and hoisin sauces, lime juice, sesame seeds, and sesame oil, and stir the mix. Put portions of the mixture on the lettuce leaves, and roll up. Put on serving plate. Serve with a chili dipping sauce if you like. (Thai-style sauces can be found in the ethnic section of your supermarket or health food store.)

* Shirataki noodles are made from the glucomannan root. They have been popular in Japan for a long time. Unlike conventional pasta, this product does not impact blood sugar levels. It tastes bland but readily absorbs the flavors of sauces and dressings. Shirataki noodles can be found in the cool case of Asian food stores or health food stores. In response to increased customer awareness, many grocery chains are now also stocking them.

Caponata

(4 servings)

1½ dozen string beans, cleaned, broken into pieces, and blanched for 3 minutes

4 green onions, chopped

1 medium eggplant, cut into 1-inch cubes

2 teaspoons salt

1 green pepper and 1 red pepper, chopped into 1-inch cubes

1 small zucchini, cut into 1-inch cubes

8 spears asparagus, cut into pieces (optional)

2 teaspoons finely minced garlic

2 tablespoons olive oil

½ cup of good-quality tomato sauce

2 tablespoons balsamic vinegar

2 tablespoons capers

Salt to taste

4 tablespoons chopped fresh basil leaves (may substitute with 2 teaspoons dried basil)

Prepare all the vegetables in advance, starting with the eggplant. Line a colander with a tea towel, cut eggplant into cubes, and sprinkle with 2 teaspoons salt. Let sit for 30 minutes. After that time, you can squeeze out the fluid. (This process will remove any bitterness from the egg-plant.) Next cut all other vegetables and set aside. In large frying pan or wok, heat the olive oil, add the onion and garlic, and briefly sauté both. Add the remaining vegetables next, and cook on medium heat until they are al dente (not mushy). Remove from stove. Add tomato sauce, vinegar, capers, and chopped basil. Put into serving bowl, and serve hot or cold. This dish can be prepared in advance, as the flavors will blend. Add a protein serving of your choice: per person you will need 5 ounces of grilled salmon or other seafood or meat.

Harvest Salad

(4 servings)

1 bunch baby broccoli (or regular broccoli), cut into pieces and blanched for 4 minutes

1 small head cauliflower, cut into florets and blanched for 4 minutes

2 golden beets, cooked and sliced

2 red beets, cooked and sliced

1 small red onion, thinly sliced

6 tablespoons slivered almonds or walnut pieces

¾ cup cubed goat cheese

8 hard-boiled eggs

1 large orange, peeled and cut into thin slices

Dressing

½ cup orange juice (freshly squeezed is best)

6 tablespoons olive oil

1 teaspoon finely grated lemon peel

½ teaspoon salt

Prepare all vegetables, and put into bowl. Sprinkle with slivered almonds or nuts and cubed cheese. Mix gently. Top with the halved hard-boiled eggs, and decorate with orange slices. Stir dressing in a small bowl. Pour dressing on top of salad and serve.

Dinner

Nobody wants to spend several hours slaving in the kitchen to produce a meal that is eaten up within less than half an hour. The good news is it's not necessary! Your most basic dinner choice can be a portion of chicken, fish, or other lean cut of meat that you prepare on a griddle/grill or the barbecue. Alternatively you can put meat in a slow cooker and find dinner ready to go. Complete it with a bowl of green salad or mixed vegetables—or steam some broccoli or asparagus—and set the table.

Some lunch choices also come in handy for dinner. A cool salad on a summer evening with cold previously grilled salmon and a light fruit sorbet for dessert can fit the bill very nicely—without your being chained to a stove and working overtime!

Beef Goulash

(2 servings)

1 pound cubed lean beef or bison

1 tablespoon olive oil

1 large onion

1 large tomato, diced

16 ounces water

1 gluten- and yeast-free cube of vegetable broth (or replace the water with liquid vegetable broth)

½ teaspoon salt

2 teaspoons sweet paprika

In a frying pan, heat the oil. Add the meat and onion and cook on medium heat till slightly browned. Put meat and onions into a Crock-pot, add the onion and the vegetable broth, and let cook at low heat till the meat is very tender. (Put the Crock-pot on in the morning, and dinner will be waiting for you when you come home from work.)

Serve with steamed cauliflower and broccoli.

Florentine Chicken

(2 servings)

1 large boneless chicken breast

1 tablespoon chopped fresh basil (or 1 teaspoon dried basil)

1 tablespoon grated parmigiano

4 thin slices prosciutto

1 tablespoon olive oil

2 tomatoes, cut into halves

3 chopped green onions

2 cups baby spinach leaves

Pinch of salt

Spread chicken breast flat, and top it with the basil, parmigiano, and prosciutto slices.

Fold in half, and hold the stuffed chicken breast together at the edges with a toothpick or two. Heat olive oil in frying pan, add onion and tomato slices, and put the chicken breast on top. Put lid on the pan, and cook at medium heat till the chicken is cooked through. (If you test with a fork, the juices will be clear.) Remove vegetables and chicken from pan, put on serving plate, and keep warm. Remove toothpicks from meat, and cut chicken breast into two portions. Put spinach into pan, and cover with lid, letting the leaves wilt at medium heat. Put spinach on the side of the chicken and tomatoes, and sprinkle with a bit of salt.

Egg in a Nest

(2 servings)

8 ounces lean ground beef (or ground chicken or turkey)

1 tablespoon finely minced onion

2 tablespoons egg white

½ teaspoon dried marjoram

1 pinch of salt and pepper

1 boiled egg

1 tablespoon olive oil

Mix the ground meat with the egg white and seasonings, and shape the mix into a rectangle. Put the boiled egg on top, and shape the meat around the egg to make a small meat loaf. Heat olive oil in a frying pan, and brown the meat loaf on all sides. Add a bit of water to frying pan, reduce heat, put a lid on the pan, and cook for 4 minutes so the meat is done. Remove from pan, cut into two halves, and serve with a green salad or a steamed vegetable of your choice.

Thai Red Chicken Curry

(2 servings)

8 ounces chicken breast or chicken thighs, cut into cubes

1 tablespoon olive oil or coconut oil

1 bunch of green onions, cleaned and chopped

4 stalks of celery, cut into 1-inch pieces

1 green or red pepper, cut into cubes

1 large carrot, cut into cubes

Thai Red Curry Spice mix* (Asian Home Gourmet is a good brand)

½ cup milk or coconut milk

2 tablespoons chopped cilantro leaves

Heat oil in wok or frying pan, and add the spice paste or spice mix. Add chicken pieces, and stir-fry for 2 minutes, after which you'll add the prepared vegetables. Cover with lid and cook till chicken is cooked through and vegetables are still tender-crisp. Add milk or coconut milk. Remove from heat, sprinkle with chopped cilantro, and serve.

Optional: add some extra spice with a drizzle of sweet Thai chili sauce.

*To make your own paste, use 1 clove of minced garlic, 1 teaspoon finely minced lemongrass, a pinch of salt, 1 teaspoon galangal, 1 teaspoon fish sauce (nuoc man), a pinch of cayenne pepper (or more if you want the spicing hotter), and ¼ cup pineapple juice.

Italian–Style Spaghetti Squash

(4 servings)

1 medium-size spaghetti squash

4 green onions, cleaned and chopped

1 green pepper, chopped

¾ cup shredded mozzarella cheese

2 eggs and 4 egg whites

½ teaspoon salt

1 teaspoon dried Italian herbs (or 2 tablespoons fresh basil and oregano, chopped)

2 teaspoons olive oil

2 thinly sliced tomatoes

3 tablespoons grated parmigiano

Cut spaghetti squash in half and place with the cut side down on plate with ⅓ cup water. Cover and microwave for 12 minutes till squash is tender. If you do not wish to use a microwave, bake squash in oven at 350°F till tender. Let squash cool; remove the seeds and scoop out the flesh, which will look like strands of spaghetti. In large mixing bowl, stir together squash, onions, peppers, mozzarella cheese, Italian herbs, and salt, and add the mixed eggs and egg whites.

Heat oven to 350°F. Grease an 8-inch square glass or ceramic pan with olive oil, and fill it with the vegetable mix. Top with tomato slices, and sprinkle with parmigiano. Bake till the eggs have set and the surface is slightly golden. (You may want to shield the surface with a piece of aluminum foil to prevent excessive browning.) Alternatively you can microwave the dish for about 10 minutes and run it under the broiler to add a touch of golden color.

Serve with a bowl of minced greens (arugula and spinach gives a nice mix), and add a sprinkle of olive oil and vinegar to the greens. Pomegranate seeds and a few pine nuts make a nice Mediterranean finish on the salad greens.

Lamb Chops Greek-Style

(2 servings)

2 lamb chops, about 5 ounces per chop

1 lemon

1 tablespoon olive oil

1 garlic clove, finely minced or pressed through a garlic press

1 tablespoon fresh basil, chopped

2 teaspoons fresh rosemary leaves, chopped

Sprinkle of salt

1 tablespoon olive oil

2 tomatoes, cut in half

1 medium sweet onion, cut into thin slices

2 cups green beans (fresh or frozen)

½ cup water

2 tablespoons crumbled feta cheese

Grate about 2 teaspoons of lemon peel from the lemon, squeeze out the juice, and stir together with olive oil. Add garlic and herbs, and spread the mix on the lamb chops. Let marinate for a few hours or overnight.

Heat grill, and grill lamb chops till cooked through. Sprinkle with salt according to taste. Cover and keep warm. In sauté pan, heat olive oil. Add onions and green beans, and put the halved tomatoes on top. Add water, and let cook on medium heat till beans are al dente. Remove from pan, put on a serving plate, and sprinkle tomatoes with feta cheese. Place lamb chops on the side of the vegetables to serve.

Seafood Club Med

(2 servings)

6 ounces wild salmon, cut into 2 portions

8 prawns

¾ cup shucked clams or 10 mussels

1 tablespoon olive oil

1 medium onion

2 chopped tomatoes

1 cup cubed zucchini

½ cup chopped peppers (green, red, and yellow mixed)

½ cup water

Salt and cracked pepper

1 teaspoon sweet paprika

2 tablespoons finely chopped parsley

In flat pot, heat olive oil, and add the prepared vegetables. Stir and sauté until onion looks glassy. Add fish, prawns, mussels, and water. Cover and cook on medium heat until salmon is cooked through. Remove from heat, sprinkle with salt, pepper, paprika, and parsley.

Serve with a summery salad on the side: sliced green cucumbers topped with Greek yogurt or tzatziki is an excellent match!

Tzatziki Dressing (on the side)

Tzatziki is a Greek yogurt dressing. You can find it in your supermarket, but here is a recipe to whip it up at home. It keeps well in the fridge and can be prepared in advance.

1 medium-size cucumber, cut into pieces

1 teaspoon salt

1 peeled garlic clove pressed through a garlic press

1¾ cup thick yogurt (Greek yogurt gives best results. Otherwise a fairly thick yogurt will be fine.)

2 teaspoons finely minced dillweed

1 tablespoon lemon juice

½ teaspoon ground pepper

Line colander with a tea towel or cheese cloth, put cucumber pieces into colander, and let sit for 30 minutes. Now squeeze out as much liquid as possible. (If liquid is not removed, your tzatziki will be runny!) Shred the cucumber, and in a mixing bowl mix together the shredded cucumber, finely grated garlic, yogurt, minced dillweed, lemon juice, and pepper. Flavors blend well within a few hours. This dressing can be kept in the fridge for about 3 days.

Desserts

Healthy food invites you to enjoy a large variety of tastes and textures, and desserts are also on the menu. Natural sweets include fresh fruit cups or fruit sorbets. But there is also room for biscotti, chocolate mousse, or tempting truffles. Start drooling—here come the desserts.

Tropical Temptation

(2 servings)

6 cubes of deep-frozen mango

1 peeled orange

½ peeled banana

1 tablespoon almond butter

6 ice cubes

Put all ingredients into a blender* and process till smooth and slushy. Decorate with an orange slice, and serve immediately.

*Any good blender will do, but some machines do not yield the same smooth results as a high-speed machine, and eventually the lower-power motor will give up. My Vitamix has been faithfully running for years of heavy use. The Blendtec blender also comes highly recommended.

Berry Sorbet

(2 servings)

2 cups deep-frozen berries (strawberries, blueberries or a berry mix, no sugar added)

¾ cup organic yogurt or goat-milk yogurt

Few drops liquid stevia or small amount of powdered stevia to taste

Put into blender and process till smooth. You will have to open the blender jar to stir the contents in between. (Observe safety precautions: never stick knife or mixing tool into running blender!) Serve with a dollop of whipped cream if desired.

Baked Apples

(2 servings)

2 medium-size apples (my favorite for baking is the Boskoop apple)

1 tablespoon ground almonds

2 teaspoons chopped raisins

Pinch of cinnamon and ground cloves

¼ cup orange juice

¼ cup water

½ teaspoon grated lemon peel

2 tablespoons yogurt

Few drops of vanilla stevia

Preheat oven to 350° F. Peel and, using an apple corer, remove core from apples.

Combine almonds, raisins, cinnamon, and cloves, and pack the stuffing into the cored apples. Pour orange juice and water with the grated lemon peel into a pie plate, and place apples into the plate. Bake for 20 to 30 minutes till apples have softened. (To save time, microwaving the apples for 8 minutes will give the same results.) Remove from oven, put into dessert bowls, and top each apple with a spoon of yogurt sweetened with vanilla stevia to taste.

Summer Parfait

(2 servings)

½ cup raspberries

½ cup blueberries

10 pitted cherries

¾ cup yogurt

1 teaspoon vanilla extract

Pinch of stevia

3 tablespoons slivered almonds

1 teaspoon olive oil

Optional: whipped cream (small amount), 1 tablespoon grated dark chocolate

Heat pan with oil, and toast slivered almonds till they are golden brown. Set aside. Mix yogurt with vanilla and stevia. In two parfait glasses (or dessert bowls), layer a few blueberries, 1 spoon of yogurt, and a sprinkle of toasted almonds. Continue with cherries, yogurt, and almonds. Top with yogurt, raspberries, and almonds. If you like, add a curl of whipped cream and a sprinkle of grated dark chocolate.

French Snowballs (Oeufs à la Neige)

2 servings

2 eggs

Small pinch stevia

½ teaspoon almond extract

1½ cups milk

Few drops vanilla stevia

4 sliced strawberries to garnish

Use an electric beater and a small mixing bowl to beat egg whites, stevia, and almond extract till the egg whites are fluffy and firm.

In flat casserole bring milk and vanilla stevia to a soft boil. Reduce the heat, and with a tablespoon scoop up the egg white in oval-shaped dumplings. Gently place into the simmering milk, and cook about 2 minutes on each side. Remove the finished "snowballs," and place on a plate. Remove the milk from the stove.

With a whisk beat the two egg yolks, and whisk them into the cooled-down milk. Return the pot to the stove, and cook on very low heat, stirring constantly, till the mixture has become more like custard.

Remove from heat; pour custard in a flat serving bowl or individual dessert bowls. Top with the egg-white snowballs. Garnish with sliced strawberries. Can be served warm or kept in the fridge and served cold.

Lemon Mousse

(2 servings)

1 lemon

2 eggs

Pinch of stevia

1 teaspoon unflavored gelatin

2 tablespoons boiling water

¼ cup heavy whipping cream

Squeeze the juice from one lemon, and finely grate the peel to get 1 1/2 teaspoons full.

Separate eggs. Using an electric beater, beat egg yolks, stevia, lemon juice, and lemon peel till creamy. In a separate bowl, beat whipping cream till creamy, and add egg whites. Continue to beat till the mixture forms soft peaks. Combine the egg yolk-lemon mixture and the egg white-cream mixture. Dissolve gelatin in boiling water till smooth, and gently fold into the lemon cream. Put into serving bowl or small individual bowls. Refrigerate till gelatin has set. Can be decorated with a twist of lemon peel.

You can prepare the same sunny mousse using orange peel and fresh-squeezed orange juice (of one orange)—or go ahead and experiment with two limes!

Mocha Cream

(2 servings)

⅓ cup heavy cream

2 teaspoons cocoa powder

1 teaspoon fine-ground coffee or instant coffee

Stevia to taste

1½ tablespoons warm water

1 tablespoon shaved chocolate or a few chocolate-covered coffee beans to decorate

Whip the cream until fluffy and peaks form. Dissolve the cocoa, coffee powder, and stevia in warm water, and gently fold into the whipped cream. Distribute into two dessert bowls, sprinkle with chocolate shavings or chocolate-covered coffee beans, and serve immediately.

After a light dinner, this rich dessert will have everybody satisfied. And it's one of the fastest desserts to make!

Snacks

Snacks can be a lifesaver on long days when dinner is still two hours away. They can be sustaining and nutritional on a road trip or a hike. But going to the supermarket and picking up a snack that is balanced and nourishing is another story. The flood of nutrition bars that are calling your name when you are hungry are not necessarily the best choice. If you read the ingredients and wonder about "isolated soy protein," "rice crisps," "maltitol," and a string of ingredients you cannot even pronounce, you may as well put the bar back with the rest and walk away. You also may wonder whether the bar with forty grams of protein is really what you need for a snack—it may be too much of a good thing.

If you want a nutrition bar, look for a product that comes from natural sources. There are raw organic bars that are based on nuts, dates, seeds, and cocoa, and for a quick bite to eat, these can be useful. You'll pay about two dollars per bar.

Once again, you know what you get if you do it yourself. You don't need a degree in nutrition! Common sense is all you need. To stave off hunger, a good snack should consist of a balance of protein and fat and some carbs.

Try some of the following:

- apple slices dipped in almond butter

- carrot and celery sticks and red pepper strips with hummus dip or guacamole

- four chicken breast or turkey breast slices, cherry tomatoes, and a few cubes of cheese

- a handful of walnuts and almonds (mixed) and a sliced pear

- one hard-boiled egg with two slices of ham and ten olives

- a mini caprese salad: sliced mozzarella with layers of tomato, two slices of prosciutto ham, and a drizzle of olive oil and vinegar

- two squares of dark chocolate (over 70 percent cocoa content) and a snack pack of Greek yogurt without added sugar

Small containers (like empty yogurt containers) and plastic zip bags are good to keep your snacks handy. So go ahead and pack a snack!

References

Introduction:
Somers, Suzanne. *Breakthrough: Eight Steps to Wellness*. The Crown Publishing Group, New York, US. 2008

Chapter 1:
The Framingham Heart Study: http://www.nhlbi.nih.gov/about/framingham/

Nelson, Ethel R. *Century 21 Cook Book: 375 Meatless Recipes*. Eusey Press, Leominster, MA,1974.

Ng, D.S. The Metabolic Syndrome: An Emerging Epidemic. *The Metabolic Syndrome Rounds* 1, no.1 (Sept. 2003): 1-6.

Reaven, G. Role of Insulin Resistance in Human Disease. *Diabetes* 37, no. 12 (1988):1595-1607.

World Health Organization. *Definition, Diagnosis and Classification of Diabetes Mellitus and Its Complications*. Geneva: World Health Org., 1999.

Expert Panel on Detection, Evaluation, and Treatment of High Blood Cholesterol in Adults: Executive Summary of the Third Report of the National Cholesterol Education Program (NCEP) Expert Panel on Detection, Evaluation, and Treatment of High Blood Cholesterol in Adults (Adult Treatment Panel III). *Journal of American Medical Association No.* 285 (2001): 2486-2497.

July 1, 2003 blog:
http://www.askdrray.com/obesity-and-metabolic-syndrome/

The National Cholesterol Education Program Expert Panel. *Third Report of the National Cholesterol Education Program Expert Panel on Detection, Evaluation, and Treatment of High Blood Cholesterol in Adults (ATP III)*, Nov.2002:
http://www.nhlbi.nih.gov/guidelines/cholesterol/

Chapter 2:

The New York Times Hardening of the Arteries In-Depth Report:
http://www.nytimes.com/health/guides/disease/atherosclerosis/print.html

The Framingham Heart Study:
http://www.nhlbi.nih.gov/about/framingham/

Kannel, William B. Risk Stratification of Obesity as a Coronary Risk Factor. *American Journal of Cardiology* 90, no. 7 (Oct. 2002): 697-701.

The Netherlands Epidemiology and Demography Compression of Morbidity Research Group. *Annals of Internal Medicine* 138 (Jan. 7, 2003):24-32.

My blog Jan. 1, 2003 regarding the Framingham Heart Study: http://www.askdrray.com/framingham-study-obesity-and-smoking-lead-to-loss-of-life/

Margellos-Anast, Helen, Shah, Ami M. and Whitman, Steve: Prevalence of Obesity Among Children in Six Chicago Communities: Findings from a Health Survey. *Public Health Rep.* 123(2). (Mar-Apr2008): 117–125
Free website access:
http://www.ncbi.nlm.nih.gov/pmc/articles/PMC2239321/

My Dec. 2002 blog regarding the Physicians' Health Study involving 21,414 physicians over 12.5 years summarizes that the mortality rate of obese subject in the study was 1.9-fold higher from strokes than for subjects with a normal weight:
http://www.askdrray.com/obesity-excessive-weight-a-predictor-of-high-risk-for-stroke/

National Cholesterol Education Program Expert Panel: *Third Report of the National Cholesterol Education Program Expert Panel on Detection, Evaluation, and Treatment of High Blood Cholesterol in Adults (ATP III).* Nov.2002: http://www.nhlbi.nih.gov/guidelines/cholesterol/

Chapter 3:

Davis, W., MD: *Wheat Belly. Lose the Wheat, Lose the Weight, and Find Your Path Back to Health.* HarperCollins Publishers LTD., Toronto, Canada, 2011.

August 2003 blog about the PYY peptide hormone that helps regulate our appetite:
http://www.askdrray.com/newly-detected-hormone-may-help-obesity/

Margellos-Anast, Helen, Shah, Ami M. and Whitman, Steve: Prevalence of Obesity Among Children in Six Chicago Communities: Findings from a Health Survey. *Public Health Rep.* 123(2). (Mar-Apr2008): 117–125
Free website access:
http://www.ncbi.nlm.nih.gov/pmc/articles/PMC2239321/

Chapter 4:

Willcox, Bradley. J., Willcox, Craig., and Suzuki, Makoto *The Okinawa Program*. New York: Clarkson Potter, 2001.

Read the full story about the incredible distortion of the truth regarding the perceived need to lower cholesterol levels in this website entitled "Know your fats; the oiling of America": http://www.westonaprice.org/know-your-fats/the-oiling-of-america

Sears, Barry. *The Top 100 Zone Foods*. Regan Books, Harper Collins, New York, US. 2001. Also see Dr. Sears's site: http://www.drsears.com/

Schmid, K.: Life Extension: Disease Prevention and Treatment, fifth edition. *130 Evidence-Based Protocols to Combat the Diseases of Aging*. "Chapter 39": Cholesterol management.2013.

My blog from July 2003 summarizes how fats can influence your mood: http://www.askdrray.com/food-and-mood/

University of Maryland: Omega-6 fatty acids: http://umm.edu/health/medical/altmed/supplement/omega6-fatty-acids

August 2008 blog: http://www.askdrray.com/positives-and-negatives-of-folate/

Sears, Barry *The Age-Free Zone*. Regan Books, Harper Collins, New York, US. 2000. Also see Dr. Sears's site: http://www.drsears.com/

Wiki review of low carbohydrate diets: http://en.wikipedia.org/wiki/Low-carbohydrate_diet

An overview of the Framingham Heart Study: http://en.wikipedia.org/wiki/Framingham_Heart_Study

Davis, W.: *Wheat Belly. Lose the Wheat, Lose the Weight, and Find Your Path Back to Health*. HarperCollins Publishers LTD., Toronto, Canada, 2011.

Perlmutter, David. *Grain Brain. The Surprising Truth About Wheat, Carbs, And Sugar-Your Brain's Silent Killers*. New York: Little, Brown, 2013.

Website explaining conventional "lipid theory" of hardening of arteries: http://www.ncbi.nlm.nih.gov/pubmedhealth/PMH0001224/

In depth report about hardening of arteries: http://www.nytimes.com/health/guides/disease/atherosclerosis/print.html

Davis, William. *Wheat Belly Cookbook: 150 Recipes to Help You Lose the Wheat, Lose the Weight, and Find Your Path Back to Health*. Toronto: Harper Collins, 2012.

The "choose my plate" or "food pyramid" diet: http://www.choosemyplate.gov/downloads/infographics/2013-EatTheMyPlateWay.pdf

FDA outlaws trans fats: http://www.politico.com/story/2013/11/fda-trans-fats-99526.html

Nov. 2013 blog: http://www.askdrray.com/statins-can-hurt-the-consumer/

"Other cause of wrinkles": http://www.prnewswire.com/news-releases/the-other-cause-of-wrinkles-and-a-solution-highlighted-at-9th-world-congress-of-dermatology-in-athens-greece-214106161.html

Arachidonic Acid website: http://www.marksdailyapple.com/arachidonic-acid/#axzz2mf0CGCKh

Dr. Frank Lipman: Natural Remedies For Inflammation: http://www.drfranklipman.com/natural-remedies-for-inflammation/

Cholesterol as an anti-inflammatory: http://metabolichealing.com/key-integrated-functions-of-your-body/cardiovascular/cholesterol-is-powerfully-anti-inflammatory-and-prevents-free-radical-activity/

Chapter 5:
Several exercise–related YouTube links have been placed right where the exercises are discussed in the chapters for ease of use.

Chapter 6:
Perlmutter, David. *Grain Brain. The Surprising Truth About Wheat, Carbs, And Sugar-Your Brain's Silent Killers*. New York: Little, Brown, 2013.

Chapter 7:
Perlmutter, David. *Grain Brain. The Surprising Truth About Wheat, Carbs, And Sugar-Your Brain's Silent Killers*. New York: Little, Brown, 2013.

NIH site on Women's Health Initiative:
http://www.nhlbi.nih.gov/whi/whi_faq.htm#q1

Dr. John Lee's website where you can order saliva hormone tests:
http://www.johnleemd.com/store/prod_stest.html

ZRTLaboratoy is Dr. David Zava's lab where you can order Saliva tests in the US: http://www.zrtlab.com/resources/collection-instructions

Rocky Mountain Analytical Laboratory in Calgary, AB specializes in saliva hormone tests for Canada:
http://rmalab.com/healthcare-professionals/our-tests

Dr. Lee website, bioidentical hormones:
http://www.johnleemd.com/store/news_bhrt.html

William Faloon 2008: "Dangers of Excess Estrogen In the Aging Male":
http://www.lef.org/magazine/mag2008/nov2008_Dangers-of-Excess-Estrogen-in-the-Aging-Male_02.htm

Lee, John R. *"Hormone Balance for Men: What your Doctor May Not Tell You About Prostate Health and Natural Hormone Supplementation."* 2007 by One-to-One Inc., Temecula, CA

Somers, Suzanne. *Breakthrough: Eight Steps to Wellness.* The Crown Publishing Group, New York, US. 2008

Wikipedia re. Bioidentical hormone replacement:
http://en.wikipedia.org/wiki/Bioidentical_hormone_replacement_therapy

NIH site on Women's Health Initiative:
http://www.nhlbi.nih.gov/whi/whi_faq.htm#q1

"Virginia Hopkins: Open letter to Oprah":
http://www.virginiahopkinstestkits.com/bioidenticalhormonebreast-cancer.html

Conaway, E. 2011: "Bioidentical hormones: an evidence-based review for primary care providers"
http://www.ncbi.nlm.nih.gov/pubmed/21464264

Female hormone restoration: A review of bioidentical hormone replacement with many references about its safety (a review by Life Extension for longer life):
http://www.lef.org/protocols/female_reproductive/female_hor-mone_restoration_01.htm#introduction

Morgentaler, Abraham. *Testosterone for Life: Recharge Your Vitality, Sex Drive, Muscle Mass and Overall Health.* McGraw-Hill books, New York, NY. 2008.

Chapter 8:

Xu, Qun, Parks, C.G., DeRoo, L.A., Cawthon, R.M., Sandler, D.P. and Chen, H. Multivitamin use and telomere length in women. *American Journal of Clinical Nutrition* 89 (April 2009):1857-63.

Full text (PDF):
http://ajcn.nutrition.org/content/89/6/1857.
full?sid=9aab0e13-b4d2-42ad-b44c-15cffc6771c3

Hayflick limit (Wiki citation): http://en.wikipedia.org/wiki/Hayflick_limit

About.com biology regarding mitochondria:
http://biology.about.com/od/cellanatomy/ss/mitochondria.htm

CNN Interactive: vitamin guide:
http://www.cnn.com/FOOD/resources/food.for.thought/vitamins.
minerals/faqs/vitamins.html

Sears, Barry *The Age-Free Zone*. Regan Books, Harper Collins, New
York, US. 2000. Also see Dr. Sears's site:
http://www.drsears.com/

March 17, 2013 blog: http://www.askdrray.com/
calcium-vitamin-d3-and-vitamin-k2-needed-for-bone-health/

Brownstein, David. *Iodine: Why You Need It, Why You Can't Live without It*,
4th edition. West Bloomfield, Michigan: Medical Alternatives Press, 2009.

Khan, et al. "Cinnamon Improves Glucose and Lipids of People with
Type 2 Diabetes." *Diabetes Care* 26, no.12 (2003): 3215-8.

Chapter 9:
Sears, B. *The Age-Free Zone*. Regan Books, Harper Collins, 2000.

Chapter 10:
No references

Chapter 11:
Willcox, B. J., Willcox, C., and Suzuki, M. *The Okinawa Program*. New
York: Clarkson Potter, 2001.

Index